To Andra

Wishing you the very best of success in

HIRED GUN II

BOTH BARRELS

your future!

Printed in the United States of America.
Cover Design by PSA, Inc.
ISBN (print): 978-0-9666668-0-9
ISBN (ebook): 978-0-9666668-1-6

COVER PHOTO: David McGhee Photo

Hired Gun® is a federally trademarked term owned by Robert Danger Workman and registered with the United States Patent and Trademark Office under these two federal registration numbers: 2,468,269 & 5,400,592

Published by:
Direct Media Marketing, LLC
P.O. Box 223752
Dallas, TX 75222

For Additional HIRED GUN® products, please visit:
HiredGun.us

HIRED GUN II

BOTH BARRELS

Blasting Business Politics

ROBERT WORKMAN

About the Author

Currently writing more books in the *HIRED GUN®* series, Robert is a 40-year veteran of face-to-face, day-in and day-out selling who has published numerous sales training/human development programs and spoken to thousands of sales reps nationwide and internationally.

His consistent track record as #1 in sales includes Top Producer awards in companies with 800, 300, and 100 reps, then getting fired while producing consistently superlative results and making too much money.

Robert is an entrepreneur, a connoisseur, and a raconteur who has lived with mountain lions and wolves as house pets, owned numerous exotic cars, and lives in a downtown warehouse he converted as his Dallas domicile. He's purchased Ferraris by writing single checks. He's also had his telephone turned off and his credit card seized at a gas station because he couldn't pony up the ducats.

When asked during radio interviews why he wrote the original *Hired Gun - You're #1, and Somebody Hates It,* he said it was because he was looking for career guidance of this kind for top-tier salespeople, and it didn't exist. Until now...

ENDORSEMENTS for HIRED GUN II

If you ever publish a sales book, two things will happen. One, time will pass and some information will become outdated. Two, you'll wake up at night (more than once) and realize what you should have put in the book. Bottom line, Workman didn't complain about it, he wrote a damn good book and made it better. Do yourself (and your wallet) a favor. Buy this book, read it, take notes and put what you learn into action.

— Vince Poscente - NY Times Bestselling Author - The Age of Speed

Workman provides you with the unvarnished truth about selling as a hired gun, and more importantly, how to adopt the mindset to succeed in spite of the all the roadblocks, obstacles, and other characters you'll meet along the way. Read the stories, pay careful attention to the lessons!

— Anthony Iannarino - Author of Eat Their Lunch: Winning Customers Away from Your Competition.

From the 30,000 foot views...

Attitude! This book reads as if it were the original source of that viewpoint. Bob Workman is a high performer with the drive and discipline of a Hired Gun, and he's a storyteller par excellence! This is a book for two types of people: those who live the kick-ass, take-no-prisoners lifestyle; and those who wish they could. It's also a great book for people who just really enjoy a true life business story well told. Strap on your guns and take a ride with Workman, you'll be better for it.

— Jim Cathcart, author of The Self Motivation Handbook, Relationship Selling and 17 other books. http://Cathcart.com

A great book for anyone seeking personal excellence and professional success -- in sales and in life.

— Dr. Nido R. Qubein | President High Point University
One University Parkway, High Point, NC 27268
Office: 336-841-9201 | Choose to be extraordinary!®

• • • • • • • • • • • • • • • • • • •

To the battles in the trenches...

Robert's new book is a swift kick in the pants and a must read for serious sales professionals. Old school, not p.c., great reference points and at times hilarious. He reminds every sales person how to get back to basics, be disciplined and sell, sell, sell!

— Whitney A. Walker, CEO
Anna Sova Organics

• • • • • • • • • • • • • • • • • • •

As a sales professional who has been on the top of a couple organizations I can honestly say that this is the most honest sales book I have ever read. Great job!

— Jonathan Berger
Director of National Advertising Sales - Captivate, LLC

• • • • • • • • • • • • • • • • • • •

Sales people are [often] people that failed at their first career. The climb to sales success can be difficult. Read *HIRED GUN* and discover what doesn't work, the dangers that are lurking and how to make your journey to sales success much easier.

— Larry Little
Account Executive, software sales

Books by Robert Danger Workman

HIRED GUN® - You're #1, and Somebody Hates It

HIRED GUN® II - Both Barrels - Blasting Business Politics

Tribute

Before I begin firing off metaphorical double-barreled blasts, please allow this brief but important digression from the overall theme of this book. This book is about sales as an honorable profession for the wonderful people who pursue it as a career. The HIRED GUN metaphor is just that - a symbolic likeness that represents the shocking similarities in lifestyle and career experienced by both top-tier salespeople and peacekeeping mercenaries.

Professional salespeople perform many tasks every day that put the fear of God in most people. But right here, right up front, we need to establish a clear differentiation between people who fight the daily battles in sales and peacekeepers who fight the daily battles for our literal safety and security.

We salespeople may like to think we're certified badasses in the business world but that's our world—business. It is, quite literally, "civil" as opposed to "criminal" or military. The freedoms we enjoy are provided by men and women who risk their lives for us. We civilians are fortunate to have our freedom; please don't forget those who actually protect it.

"Mere words" are difficult to come by that describe the respect and admiration I have for the intrepid people who comprise every branch of our military and our domestic first responders like police, fire, EMS, and homeland security. For each negative storyline in the media that examines one of their actions under an electron microscope, there are hundreds of other successful heroic actions accomplished by these true heroes every day that we never see, never hear about, never know about.

These are truly the Unsung Heroes of our culture who lay down their lives to protect our freedoms. That is the most real world of all realities. To us, daily life is taking off work early to go watch a baseball game; to them, it's life and death, protecting our homeland, protecting our citizens. What we do in our civilian lives pales in comparison to the courageous deeds of these men and women every day.

You think you have a horrible day because one of your deals went south? Think about the soldier whose vehicle gets blown up by an improvised explosive device. Think about the police officers gunned down escorting participants in what should have been peaceful demonstrations.

We might suffer the slings and arrows of outrageous misfortune, but those are "attacks" on us in a civil environment that involve feelings and words, not bullets. We can still go to our favorite bars to drown our sorrows in tall, cool drinks on the way to our safe, secure homes. So please appreciate those who voluntarily risk their lives so you can enjoy your rights and freedoms.

I am as serious as a train wreck about the subject matter in this book, but we both know that all these Hired Gun-isms are lighthearted metaphors. They serve to illustrate some of the characteristics, behaviors, and career consequences that salespeople and mercenaries have in common. I would never even conceive of the thought of placing myself on equal footing with the real paladins in our culture who physically protect us all, and these metaphors are not intended to denigrate the work or sacrifices of first responders.

Preface

If I didn't know that the quote below is an interchange between Henry Fonda and Dorothy Malone in the 1959 western, *Warlock,* I'd think it was the conclusive hiring interview between a top-tier sales rep and HR. Welcome to the life of a Hired Gun, a top revenue producing professional salesperson:

> Fonda:
> You don't approve of me do you, Miss...?
>
> Malone:
> Marlow, Jesse Marlow.
> It doesn't matter much.
> I'm in the minority.
>
> Fonda:
> You won't be in the minority long, Miss Marlow.
> People generally begin to resent me.
> I don't mind it when it happens; it's part of the job.
> But it will happen.
> I come here as your salvation at a very high wage.
> I establish order, ride roughshod over offenders.
> At first, you're pleased because there's a good deal less trouble.
> Then a very strange thing happens.
> You begin to feel I'm too powerful.
> You begin to fear me.
> Not me, but what I am.
> And when that happens, we should have had full satisfaction from one another. It'll be time for me to leave.

Malone:
You speak as though from great experience, Marshal.
Has this happened many times?

Fonda:
Yes ma'am, Miss Marlow.
In very many towns.

The Hidden Agendas of Oz

Remember *The Wizard of Oz*? The plot centers around Dorothy and her three friends: The Scarecrow, Tin Man, and Cowardly Lion. All they want are the answers to a few simple questions. But what do they get? Intimidation, manipulation, and the assignment of a dangerous and unrealistic challenge from an unseen autocrat, The Wizard of Oz.

When the intrepid quartet returns to The Wizard with proof of their accomplishment, what's the first thing he does? He tries to back out of his deal with them. Of course, when Toto slides back the curtain, we see that this fearful persona is really just a short, dumpy old guy hiding behind a chintzy shower curtain while he blasts his overbearing commands through the instruments of a steampunk control booth.

There is no real power behind The Wizard, only his phony words. As a matter of fact, it turns out that Dorothy's fantasy *Wizard of Oz* is based on a traveling con man, Professor Marvel.

The Wizard's curtain is as flimsy as the phony curtain of corporate elitist obfuscation I will tear down for you in *HIRED GUN II*. What weapon does The Wizard wield to create his superficial barrier? Words that are as meaningless as the hot air he uses to power his balloon up and out of Oz.

Together, we'll blast through the corporate geek jargon manufactured to obscure what's really happening in your company: reduced commission plans, reduced territories, increased quotas, firings of top producers, sales meetings, non-sales meetings—and more meetings, sales projections, sales forecasts, check-in calls from management, role play sessions, activity reports, expense reports, report reports, and any other micromanagement sales **impediments** Suits and managers can conjure up.

> impediment (n.)
>
> c. 1400, from Old French, *empedement* or directly from Latin *impedimentum* "hindrance," from *impedire* "impede," **literally "to shackle the feet"**
>
> *The Online Etymology Dictionary*

I'm not going to just tear the curtain down. I'm blasting a hole in it first with *Both Barrels*. Then I'm tearing it down.

Table of Contents

Introduction

I love, respect, and admire sales people.

HIRED GUN II provides an inside perspective of a sales career and industry politics unlike anything else you will read. This book is not about how to sell. It's about adversity that happens when you're ultimately successful in your sales endeavors, and how to make it all work in your favor. This is based on direct experience from four decades of my personal, firsthand work as a top revenue producer in several different sales positions, companies, and industries.

If you're at the top of your game for whatever you do, read this book—it shows you how to stay there.

If you're the top sales rep in your outfit, especially read this book—it's written for you.

If you aspire to become the top rep in your outfit, read this book—you'll learn what lies ahead.

If you want to know what to expect in your life and career as your company grows from its success, read this book.

If you want to learn how to identify and maximize your single most valuable asset, read this book.

If you want to learn how to identify and maximize your single greatest power, read this book.

If you need to know what to do now, because you're great at your job and YOU'VE JUST BEEN FIRED—immediately skip ahead to the chapter, "Fired Gun".

And if you're a professional salesperson who's afraid to say so for fear of negative connotations about your chosen career, you need to read this book—or you need to get another job.

You and I both know this: whatever trendy new sales impediments the Suits invent to preoccupy your time and energy, at the end of each month they all have one question:

"Is that deal coming in today?"

That's the only sales metric that counts. That's the bottom line.

As your month end nears and the Suits chirp away in your ears, you might feel like the beleaguered World Champion and Formula One racing driver, Kimi Raikkonen.

As Raikkonen delivered the first Formula One victory ever for Team Lotus, his pit management crew badgered him relentlessly over his headphones about his driving tactics. His response is now part of racing lore:

Leave me alone. I know what I'm doing.

—Kimi Raikkonen,
Grand Prix of Abu Dhabi

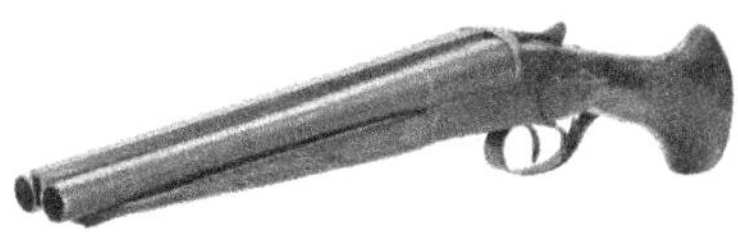

Shinda

You will see this term used repeatedly throughout this book.

It is a Japanese word for "Dead" (wordhippo.com), which was brought to my attention by one of my most highly prized friends and colleagues, the inimitable Mo Fo Bro.

I employ its use and meaning here to symbolize the demise of companies that predictably grow too big for their own britches, over expanding and over managing themselves into oblivion after soaring to incredible heights of success.

死んだ

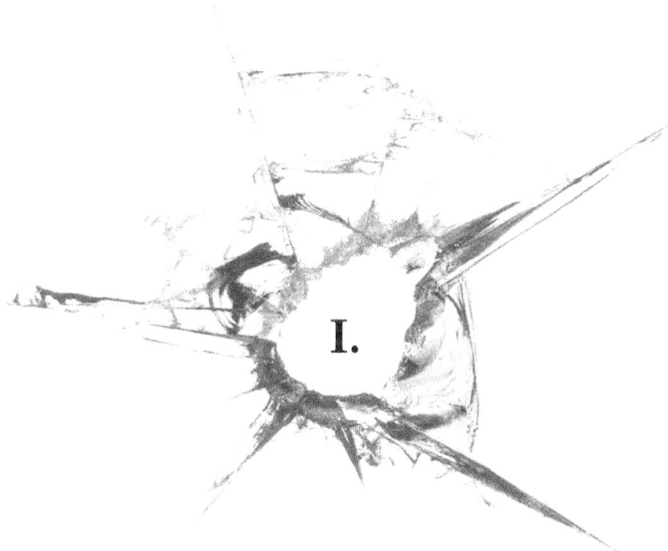

I.

Both Barrels

In which we examine the purpose and attitude of this book and its value to you

The original *HIRED GUN* received quite an honor when Brian Tracy, the eminent global expert on sales training, wrote, “This is a great, hard-hitting book, full of punchy examples that tell it like it *really* is in the fast-paced world of sales and sales management.”

This Is the Real Deal

HIRED GUN II teaches you what comes next with: 1) your career in sales, 2) your success in sales, 3) securing your personal and professional identities, and 4) gaining control over your own life. If it has to be categorized, I suppose it’s a “things you don’t learn in school” book.

This is a firsthand account of what I learned over four decades as a successful career salesman, sales manager, sales Suit, entrepreneur, and business owner who was in the field, prospecting, making calls, setting appointments, making presentations, and closing deals. I performed all of these actions in person in outside sales, and over the phone or via online demos in inside sales to small business owners, police chiefs, fire chiefs, ad agency account execs, boards and board chairmen, CEOs, VPs, and 37-person decision groups. In the process, I formed genuine, enduring relationships with almost all of them.

This is based on my professional experiences as a guy who's been there, sold that, excelled, flourished, got shot, survived, healed, peeled off the bandages, got back in the game, excelled, and flourished again, got shot again, got over it, and proved in repeated fashion over the years that indeed...

Living well is the best revenge.

— **Law of the Hired Gun** - with gratitude to George Herbert

Why do I tell you all that? Only to make this point: do you want to learn from somebody who thinks about it or talks about it—or from a guy who's done it?

This book provides proven, experience-based solutions that help you gain confidence and knowledge so slings or arrows—from outside your company or from within—don't faze or deter you. It shows you how to maximize the power of your freedom of choice, and most important, how to take control of your own life before someone else does it for you.

So, What's in It for You?

I was very fortunate to befriend some of the greatest Masters of Sales at an early age and learn this marvelous craft from them. As you get to know them in these pages, I hope you will benefit from their teachings as much as I did.

Awesome professionals like the late, great Joseph J. Charbonneau, Roy the Boy, Cy Young, Mickey Spillane, and others were generous enough to help hone my skills while I developed what would become my life's work. Joe was one of the most sought-after speakers and sales trainers on the planet, delivering more than 220 speaking engagements a year. Roy was simply the best salesman and best sales manager I ever knew. Cy taught me how to become recognized as an expert in my industry through my outbound marketing initiatives. And Mickey, one of the greatest mystery writers of all time, sold an estimated 200 million books. He taught me more about successful writing in one extended lunch than I learned in six years of college.

My mission is to bring to you the teaching and coaching of these world leaders, along with the knowledge I gained studying more than 200 books, writing 20 learning modules in sales, sales management, and personal development, and speaking to thousands of people on sales-related subjects. I wrote this book for career sales reps (and all business professionals) who are in the trenches selling day-in and day-out, face-to-face or over the phone.

Why? Because things like this you don't get in school.

First of all, everything in this book is true. These are first-hand accounts of things I've done or seen myself—no hearsay, no rumor, no innuendo.

It's from these experiences that I internalized our greatest assets: a strong sense of identity or self worth, the power of choice, and the irreplaceable value of world-class mentors.

Here is a partial list of takeaways from this book:

- **Know that sales offer the best Return on Investment (ROI) of any career.**
- **Build your own bullet-proof self-concept, self-image, and identity awareness.**
- **Leverage your greatest power—the power of choice.**
- **Choose between champions versus coaches as your mentors.**
- **Forecast the stages of a company's evolution as it relates to sales.**
- **Identify the telltale signs that the time is coming for you to decide: stay, adapt, overcome or...leave.**
- **TAKE CHARGE WHEN YOU GET FIRED.**

First - Congratulations on your decision for a career in sales! You've chosen wisely. Sales has the best Return on Investment of any career choice. It gives you the opportunity to be of service to your clients and company and to reap the rewards of your contributions.

Second - This isn't limited to salespeople. It's for business professionals: Bosses, CEOs, Suits, sales managers, and salespeople. It deals with a much broader scope than sales training.

HIRED GUN II identifies and exposes agendas set into motion within your organization before, during, and after your sales calls that are more important than closing any one particular deal, even your biggest deal. Because *you* are the biggest deal.

There are a lot of books and white papers you can read about sales, and if you miss one, just wait. Another one will be along any minute. Unfortunately, I've come to learn this is the only book that "tells it like it really is in the fast-moving world of sales and sales management."

A little after one company's exciting five-year run as one of the *Wall Street Journal's* "Top Ten Fastest Growing Companies," I ran into Our Former Boss of more than 1,000 employees at a social event. The first thing he said was, "Well, Robert, that was a wild ride for 60 months, wasn't it?" What did he mean? I'll tell you:

Get Ready for a Wild Ride

One of the chief lessons I learned from my mentors is to get to the bottom line. So, let's get down to it.

Slow-Pitch Softball Warm Up Question: Why don't salespeople receive pay raises?

Everybody else throughout your organization receives an increase in pay usually based on some length of tenure or a collection of outstanding achievements. You brought in the Biggest Deal in the History of All Time for your company last month. Beyond your scheduled commission for the deal, did you get a raise in your base pay rate or commission rate as a reward for your achievements?

Nope.

Usually the Suits' response is, "So, what have you done for me lately?" Or they say, "If you want to earn more, sell more."

Let me ask the Suits this: Do accountants earn more if they add up more numbers? Does the IT staff earn more if they process more bytes that month? Does the front desk person make more if they handle more phone calls or visitors? Do managers make more if they produce and submit more reports?

Do the Suits tell your accountants, if you want to make more, add up more columns of numbers? Do they tell your IT department, if you want to make more, create more GUI interfaces or build more platforms? Do they tell your front desk person, if you want to make more, answer the phone more times or greet more visitors? Do they tell your managers, "Please, give me more reports, and we'll pay you more?"

No. Those positions normally receive pay rate increases after marking a certain amount of time within your company. I mean, fair's fair. If a staff person gets a 10 percent raise in their pay rate after three years, why doesn't a sales rep get a 10 percent raise in their base pay rate or a 10 percent raise in their commission percentage rate after the same period of time?

You've been the star sales rep for five years at your company. Are you seeing any increases in your base pay or commission percentages? If you do, count your blessings, and give Your Boss a sincere handwritten note of appreciation.

Unfortunately, in every one of the many companies for which I've worked, I've not been able to write that note because that's never happened. As a matter of fact:

The longer you stay in one sales position in one company, the more time they have to figure out how to reduce the money you make.

— Law of the Hired Gun

FOR EXAMPLE:

A sly corporate ploy to control the income of a successful sales rep is for the Suits to tell you they want to reward your exceptional work with an offer to move into a position in management, which is a demotion in disguise. You're tempted with a new title and a base slightly higher than the one you currently receive, but all your accounts and commissions have to be turned over to the house. The upshot: you do a lot of work with spreadsheets in a tiny office, and in the end, you make a lot less money.

This happened to me a couple of times. I turned the first offer down, and the company accused me of "not being a team player." I took the second offer but only after I had a signed agreement that I would keep my two largest accounts and full standard sales commissions for both, on top of the manager's base pay plus an override on sales volume.

Never accept more job responsibility without a raise.

— Law of the Hired Gun

Follow-Up Question: Are you paid the same base salary rate and/or the same commission rate for new business as the newbie? Again, in every company I've ever been part of, this is the case.

But you say, "Aw, the hell with it," go back to work, and you sell more, and you earn more.

Your clients love you because you do a great job for them. You continue to work through the inherent challenges of sales and enjoy a nice home, drive a nice car, wear nice clothes, take nice vacations, and use nice equipment and gadgets to do your job better.

Then one day, you walk into work and get fired.

Of course, HR justifies the termination by citing an email joke you forwarded to someone, a cartoon you drew, or a note you wrote. Or something you said in a bistro on a caye 30 miles off the coast of Belize on vacation that somehow got picked up by a company drone or a satellite 25,000 miles above Earth.

It doesn't matter what reason they give. If they want to whack you, they will figure out a way to do it. (And believe me, when you start earning "too much money," they want to whack you. More on this in the chapter *Fired Gun.*)

The Hired Gun Gets Shot

I was once heavily recruited to return to a company of more than 100 sales reps. The day I accepted this position, I had to turn down a different opportunity offered by a huge international technology company that paid a six-figure base and a very lucrative pay plan. Phone calls from two sales managers and three sales reps persuaded me to return. Three months after my first day, I became the #1 top revenue producer. No brag, just fact, and for this reason: a few months after that, I was fired.

I received a company-wide email from the CEO in New York about the group hugs he recommended to all employees to help deal with the terrorist attacks of September 11, 2001. (Really, not kidding, it was not a suggestion, almost a mandate. Our fearless leader wanted us all to set time aside from our work to have group hugs!)

I forwarded it to my direct report Suit and said I preferred to maintain my focus and do the job I was hired to do, which was to produce revenue to benefit the company because at the end of the month he wasn't going to come to me for my number of group hugs but for how much revenue I delivered. *Whoosh!* Down the hall to HR.

You get fired, and you're searching for a new sales job. The main thought going through your mind is, "I was doing a great job. Why did this happen?" (Or, "Why did this happen again?")

Your previous company puts a newbie in your slot, conscripts your accounts as "house accounts," and turns them over to the rookie who makes a lot less money. The newbie gladly laps up the reduced commissions on these new "found" accounts.

And so, the company whacks its top hunter-gatherer and replaces you with a farmer. A farmer is an account manager who can't make the calls, access the true decisionmakers for presentations, or close deals like you can. The farmer merely maintains the momentum on deals you hunted, gathered, closed, and dragged back into the tent.

At this stage, your company doesn't want to pay a high income like yours. It wants to sustain the company's cash flow until it's sold, merged, or taken public with an IPO. In the meantime, it needs to show profits that are as high as possible for any potential suitors or investors.

One means of showing increasing profits is by decreasing overhead like sales commissions. This shows higher profit margins on your accounts by reducing how much commission gets paid on those accounts. That difference transfers nicely to the company's bottom line profit margins on their spreadsheets. Add to that the savings on more accounts your company racks up when it fires yet another top-tier rep, then another, and another.

Sales War Stories

Just like you, I have a ton of sales war stories. A few sneaked in here to serve as real-life illustrations of some specific power points; I hope they are at least mildly entertaining.

But please keep in mind I am adamantly opposed to the notion of boasting about sales deals as $uccess $tories. Nobody ever has the fastest car on the road, and nobody ever sold The Biggest Deal in the History of All Time. But some war stories are just, fun.

Gratuitous War Story Alert

Before I walked The Last Mile of this company's hallways toward HR, I was the happy recipient of a fun monthly award for sales production: a brand-new European convertible sports car.

It was such a sweet ride that even though it was December, I constantly drove with the top down. After a few days, I noticed a distinctly un-auto type smell. It didn't make sense. The top was always down, and there was no mentionable odor lingering in my garage.

Finally, a cold winter day crept into Dallas. I put up the top for the first time and turned on the heater. A few blocks away, warm air kicked in, a stench filled the cockpit, and I felt like I was being asphyxiated. I was forced to pull over, put the top down, and drive in misty, freezing temperatures all the way home.

I searched the car and found nothing. But now my garage smelled like something crawled inside it and died. I reached deep into the empty trunk and wrestled with the new and unused convertible top cover until I finally pried it out. The smell that greeted me was beyond wretched.

Beneath the convertible top cover and tucked neatly into the deepest recesses of the trunk laid a pair of plastic wrapped raw Cornish hens. They had been planted there for well over a week and finally chose that day to announce their presence. And I laughed out loud.

Even after the removal of these decaying fowl, their odor so permeated the car's fabric and leather that it lingered for weeks. Wherever I drove it, I parked the little car with the trunk lid open, anything to help air it out.

Did I say one word about it back at the office? Of course not. The only people with the car's keys were the sales managers who controlled its monthly allocation based on final sales results. This was their way of welcoming me back, with a smelly nod to the myriad practical jokes I played on *them* in the past. I took it as a compliment to be the target of such a subtle and effective practical joke.

That is, until I got whacked a couple months later for not playing Corporate Simon Says.

Humans Sell to Humans - This Book is Based on Human Nature

Like most successful salespeople, I know a little bit about a lot of things, and there are a few things about which I know a lot. My observations are rooted in truths that have withstood many tests over extended periods of time because they are based on human nature.

As the great philosophers and authors of literature (Aristophanes, Horatio, Juvenal, William Shakespeare, Alexander Pope, John Dryden, Jonathan Swift, Mark Twain, Evelyn Waugh, and Tom Wolfe, to name a few) have illustrated in their works throughout thousands of years, this is the bottom line:

Human nature does not change.

— Law of the Hired Gun

We do the same things, feel the same emotions, and laugh at the same jokes today that human beings have done, felt, and laughed at for the past millennia. For example, *Philogelos*, the world's oldest known joke book, was written in Greek about 1,500 years ago. In his 2018 *Reader's Digest* article, "What's the Actual 'Oldest Joke in the Book?' We Just May Have Found It," Andy Simmons pulls out several jokes that are all still relevant and tells them as if he's in a Pompeii lounge act.

This is the joke he saves for last:

A doctor talks to a patient.

Patient: "Doctor, whenever I get up after sleep, I feel dizzy for half an hour, then I'm all right."

Doctor: "Then wait half an hour before getting up."

Rim shot!

With all the current TED talks, videos, websites, sales symposiums, high-priced consultants, and sales-related books that have come out since the original *HIRED GUN*, the question that persists in my head is: why are things so screwy for salespeople?

Your Suits want you to make more outbound calls to prospects, schedule more online demos, sell bigger deals, and sell more of them, but why is it so difficult to do more than what you're already doing? Why are salespeople not earning at a higher rate than they did last year or the last two or three or four years?

And BTW: why is that company that you used to work for not around anymore?

During each one of my successful assignments in sales, I observed the numbers of employees in the companies I worked for double. I also saw a swamp of PROCESS requirements and other muddy issues that followed as a result of the expansion's new layers of management.

Daily we received a call from a manager who wanted to go over the same things we went over with them or a different manager the day before, and the day before, and—yes—the day before that. The cubicles shrunk from offices to typical six-foot Boofs to five-foot Boofs to little carrels adjacent to each other with paper-thin barriers. I recently spoke to a former colleague and asked how he liked his new digs after his company moved again due to expansion.

"I look to my left and see five earholes," he said.

WIIFM? ("What's in It for... You?")

One big reason why you want to read this book is so you can develop the skill of knowing when to saddle up and ride on for your next new sales adventure. Because if you don't do it for yourself, it will be done for you.

When I wrote the original *HIRED GUN*, I gave the unfinished manuscript to two people I respected: the late Joseph J. Charbonneau, my sales and business mentor, and my dad, a scientist, medical doctor, submarine school instructor, and US Navy Captain.

Joe was a lifelong salesman. He trained thousands of salespeople, and he consulted with many huge companies to improve the performance of their people and increase their commitment to excellence. He also had been a part of businesses from the inside-out for decades, and had studied hundreds of books on sales and management. Joe said, "This is great. I've never seen another book like this!" and gave me the great honor of writing its *Foreword*.

Every business owner and executive I knew admired my dad for his global scientific achievements and expertise overseeing life-threatening deep sea diving operations. This time, as I handed him my manuscript, I asked him to consider something different for a moment. I asked him to imagine that his job was to somehow convince strangers to give him money for his business. Here's the phone, Dad. Get started.

I asked him to imagine that this is what he does daily to earn an income. More important, he has to create not just enough revenue to pay his own way but enough on top of that to pay all the people in his company and cover overhead, production, shipping, accounting, postage, HR, IT, rent, and so on.

He has to do that every single month or the company's bills don't get paid, and the other employees don't get paychecks. And by the way, there are competitors in his same industry out there who are well trained to compete against him for the same funds.

My dad said, "I didn't know sales was so stressful."

Why Hired Gun II?

Why am I writing this book, after I thought I pretty much said it all in the original *HIRED GUN*?

While the original *HIRED GUN* exposed unspoken truisms about the sales profession, *HIRED GUN II* is a massive update that delves deeply into serious issues faced by salespeople today and provides common sense, real-life solutions based on many years of *mano-a-mano* experiences.

This book takes up where the original left off with significant detailed examples to help you readily identify exactly what's going on around you in your job and in your company.

Call Me Icarus

My mentor, Joe Charbonneau, called me into his office one day and told me, "I've been studying you. I just want you to know, by the time you're 30, you're going to be illegal," his way of paying me his ultimate personal compliment. True to Joe's prophecy, I was indeed on my way up and getting all those wonderful things a person accumulates when they taste their first financial success.

At 29, I was doing all right as a fledgling writer turned fledgling sales guy. I broke the $100K barrier ($225,000 ***in 2018 money***), then broke the $200K barrier ($446,000 in 2018) at age 30. Three years later, I donned a Sales Suit and owned 7 percent of a company that earned $35 million in today's money in our first 10 months. I thought it would last forever, and pictured retiring by age 45 and working my cattle ranch.

Then our vulture capitalists sold us out to our competition. We all got whacked so our enemies could put their own people in our places, in our office, in our building, in the company that we founded.

Just for a moment, walk a couple feet in my moccasins. Everything I earned in 33 years was gone in about 33 days: a 70-acre ranch, three-story antebellum house, 40 registered Texas Longhorn cattle, three horses, wolves, dogs, trucks, trailers, and four cars (Ferrari, Mercedes, Chevy 454 pickup truck). Oh, and my wife left as well. Even my phone was turned off because I couldn't pony up funds for the $50 tab. Fortunately, I still had some leftover credit cards, but even one of these was taken out of my hands at a gas station on a cold and rainy February night.

And this was only my first reversal of fortune.

But every time I got knocked down, I reached deep inside for a gut check, and figured out a way to soar back up to those wonderful heights. Then I got shot down again and shot back up to the top. Then I got hit by flak and took a nosedive before I soared up again!

Yes sir, Boss, it has been one wild ride!

So What?

This one's for you.

If I learned and mastered sales then successfully applied it, so can you. It was not at all in my blood to be a salesman. My immediate family wasn't even a business-oriented family; they were mostly academics, scientists, and military people. I had to learn it all firsthand.

A big reason I was able to be successful at different companies in vastly different industries was because all the things I learned about sales and business leadership are transferable skills. My goal is to transfer as many of them as possible to you.

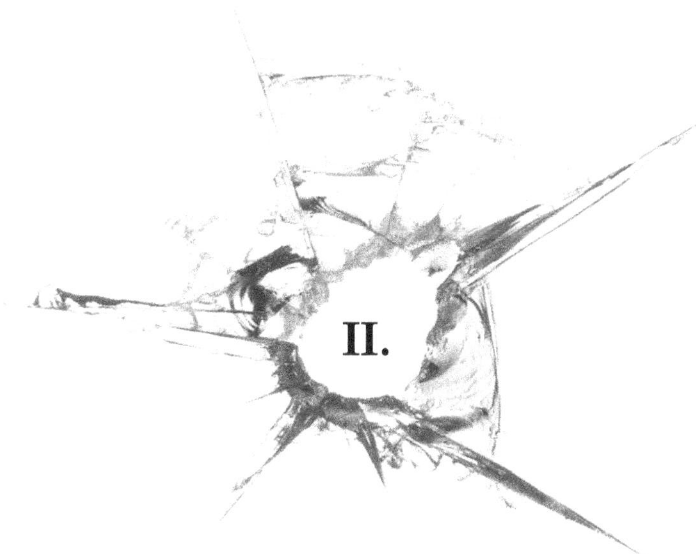

II.

Are You Playing Poker with a Dead Man's Hand?

In which we examine the ironic events that occur when you strike it rich due to your excellence in sales

---

If you aren't currently reporting directly to the person who either hired you or promoted you, you're gambling with your career while holding a dead man's hand.

— Law of the Hired Gun

You may be one of the baddest assed professionals in your business. You may be the latest *wunderkind,* whiz kid, rock star, or the most unruffled seasoned veteran.

It doesn't matter. You think the full house of jacks and sevens you're holding is a winning hand.

But that is the original dead man's hand, known long before Wild Bill Hickok, and his aces and eights. The hands in your company's game are all dealt by the Suits, and the hand they're holding has four aces. They're waiting to lay it on the felt with a cat-eating grin after they so smoothly deal your seemingly pat full house. Let's examine the reasons.

First, whoever hired or promoted you did so because your ideology matched theirs. You're close enough in your thinking for them to risk their company (if it's the owner) or their career reputation (if it's a Suit) by providing you the opportunity to earn a living working for them.

This relates to your ability to perform necessary tasks, and also to implement new strategies and tactics that develop your position. Performing well helps you keep your job, increase your income, or be promoted. (Getting along personally with your coworkers also helps!)

Simple? Business 101? Of course. Then it shouldn't be difficult to fathom that...

...all these circumstances change when the critical person who hired you or promoted you moves on.

Let's say it's Your Boss. If you're the right-hand man to Your Boss when someone comes along, ponies up the ducats and buys her out, take notice. She's hit her target, built a business, sold it, and left the company—exit, stage left. She quite rightfully pockets the proceeds, buys you a drink, waves adios, then puddle jumps to Hawaii.

You better have a golden parachute in place because it probably won't be long before you're given the choice to leave or be ever so gently nudged, nudged, and nudged again out the door.

Let's say you're a sales manager. You push your way through the company's double glass doors the first day of the next month and find a new Vice President of Sales hanging pictures in her windowed corner office. It's probably a good time to renew auld acquaintances and take charge of your new direction before someone else shows it to you.

Or, you're a #1 sales rep. You earn more than everyone in your company, except Your Boss. You've been the top revenue producer several years in a row. You drive a high-toned European convertible, wear fine clothes, and live in the community rated highest on your residential real estate map so if you have kids they can go to good schools.

Your sales manager of several years accepts a position in another company that provides a more upscale entrepreneurial opportunity. This is the person who consistently steps up to fade the heat on your behalf so you can focus on production instead of playing petty parlor politics. This is a really good professional sales manager, and you miss the comradeship more than the management. You're sorry to see the departure of the professional who has more than likely also become your friend.

But you tell yourself that you're fine. You're *made* in The Company. You produce huge revenues and have for years. Besides, you're almost as sacred to your clients as you are to your own accounts receivable department.

You persuade yourself that there's no way your company can afford to endanger the strong relationships (and the consistent revenue stream) you've forged with the client base you built.

Lo and behold, the newly appointed ruddy-faced Executive Vice President Sales Suit, who originally came into the company as an engineer, appoints a fellow whiskey-faced boozer buddy as your new sales manager. Your new incoming sales manager has absolutely no sales management experience, but he got to know the Sales Suit in a rush-hour delaying watering hole.

You think it's ridiculous but you're a champion; you have a job to do. You don't let it bother you. You believe you're in control of your own destiny.

You've established a track record of strong results. You're focused on your job, and think that surely the people in the ivory tower will see the folly of this move. You'd almost bet money that the new EVP will get called in for a sit-down with Your Boss about his poor selection for the sales manager position to replace the excellent one who left.

Within 60 days, the Black Widow of HR knocks on your office door. She informs you your position has been discontinued and offers you a generous severance package. During your exit interview, which is over the phone with the new guy, the Black Widow sits across your desk as The Fool opens with an indication of his total lack of skills reading people and situations.

"How are you doing!?!" he gleefully asks.

And believe it or not, when you reply that you've had better starts to your day, The Fool immediately follows up with, "How are you doing!?!" True story.

Nothing personal. Just business. New positioning in the company's new direction. Thank you for all the new accounts with their annual revenue streams, but your position just doesn't exist anymore.

Fine. Take the $40,000 severance package and thumb your nose *adios* as you put the building in the rearview mirror of your Testarossa.

WAAAAAAAH!!! I can hear the cries of the group-hug HR types now:

"This doesn't happen!"

"You're being negative!"

"It only turns out that way if you expect it to!"

What a crock. This is the truth. I know it. I've seen it. I've been whacked by it. You know it, too. And so do they. But they have to justify their jobs. *We don't. We do it daily with our sales production.*

So What?

Why does this happen to top-producing sales reps? Is there anything you can do about it? Let's take a look at who you are and what makes you tick. Let's delve into the *Anatomy of a Hired Gun.*

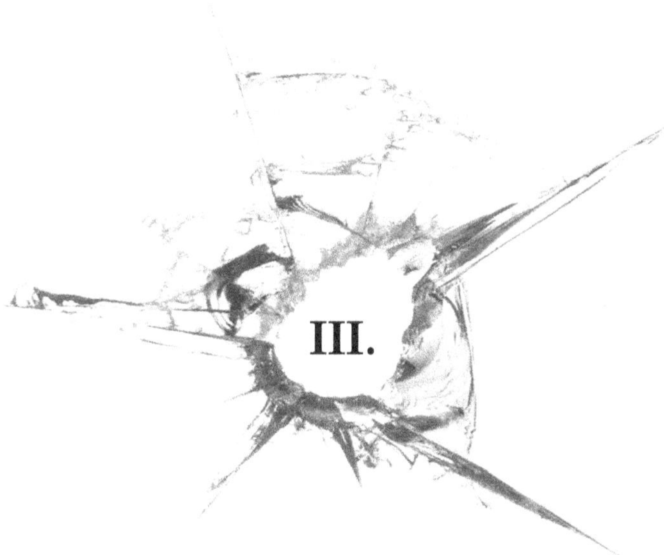

III.

Anatomy of a Hired Gun

In which we explore the character, traits, skills, lifestyle, choices, pitfalls, and self-salvation of a high-performance salesperson — namely, you

It's the first day at your new sales position. You sit at your new naked desk and look out the window into the early morning darkness. You think, "Life is one hell of a challenging trip. I was successful there. Now I need to be successful here. Let's go!"

You have a lot to learn ahead of you, and wish you had five years' experience before you make your first call. You consider the things that you know, and don't know about your new business and new company. On the verge of your very first phone call to a prospect, you feel a little doubt. You wonder, "Can I do it again? Do I have the energy and desire? Do I have the confidence?" If you didn't, you wouldn't be human.

This growing company needs revenue, sales, and the most professional rainmakers it can afford. That's why they hired *you*. You're brought in to be the new Big Dog. Now, BE the new Big Dog. Don't talk about it. Show it and perform.

You look at your reflection in the window, and it hits you. "Hell, yes!" You make the call.

1 - You're a Hired Gun

A Hired Gun is a highly recruited professional who, like Henry Fonda in *Warlock*, "come(s) here as your salvation at a very high wage." In business, that salvation is the revenue needed to sustain the life of a company.

- **Hired Guns write their own bulletproof personal identity and sense of self-worth.**
- **Hired Guns care about achieving results more than gaining the favor of other people.**
- **Hired Guns work hard, work smart, and enjoy the fruits of those labors.**
- **Hired Guns stick to their guns and persevere in the face of adversity.**
- **Hired Guns do what other people cannot or will not do.**
- **Hired Guns don't talk about it; hired guns do it.**

- Hired Guns don't make the same mistake twice.
- Hired Guns control life and life's circumstances.
- Hired Guns face challenges with enthusiasm.
- Hired Guns take calculated risks.
- Hired Guns write specific goals.
- Hired Guns are decisive.
- Hired Guns do whatever it takes to get the job done.

When the challenge and the job at hand is achieved, a Hired Gun saddles up and rides on to the next one.

2 - You're an Unconscious Competent

How can we tell a Hired Gun when we meet one? What inner characteristics does a Hired Gun embody beyond the outward visual signs of quality professional business attire, equipment, and attitude?

Hired Guns are dedicated to being the best they can possibly be as human beings and as professionals. They are not concerned with being the #1 salesperson. They are concerned with being #1 as a human being and with putting 100 percent of who they are into everything they do, every day. They invest in themselves personally and professionally, and continually grow. And often, this results in being the best at what they do.

When they focus on their role in their job, they gladly pay the price to rise to the pinnacle of their occupation. You may be familiar with the "Four Stages of Learning Any New Skill," which was developed at Gordon Training International, a world-renowned human relations training organization. In terms of sales skills, a Hired Gun becomes what is known as an "**Unconscious Competent**." The other stages are:

Conscious Competent
Conscious Incompetent
Unconscious Incompetent

For example, I'm an unconscious competent in a sales situation, but there is no doubt I'm a conscious incompetent when it comes to investing in the stock market. (I have absolutely mastered the practice of buying high and selling low.)

<u>Unconscious Competents:</u> Are beyond knowing that they understand how to do their jobs. They execute. They know what they're doing so well they don't have to think about it. They can draw, fire, and hit their targets blindfolded. They've been there so often, at such a high level with such success, that they've internalized the skills necessary to become the #1 professional in their field. And they are fun to observe in action.

<u>Conscious Competents:</u> Know that they know how to do their jobs. They are true high achievers who constantly work to learn how to perform better. They are closely focused on the mechanics that drive their actions through their diligent efforts to improve.

<u>Conscious Incompetents:</u> Know that they don't know how to do their jobs. Most often, these are new employees who know that there's a lot for them to learn. They often seek out people in the company to help them grow in their jobs. They're often good people who want to do a good job; they just haven't learned how to, yet.

<u>Unconscious Incompetents:</u> Don't know that they don't know how to do their jobs.

To witness a vivid illustration of the staggering performance gap between an unconscious competent and a conscious competent, we cut to a gunfight scene in the movie, *Butch Cassidy and the Sundance Kid*. When the outlaws try to go straight and interview for honest jobs as payroll guards, The Boss wants to see their shooting prowess.

The Boss handles the Sundance Kid's pistol and examines it:

Boss:
Fairly nice-looking piece. Can you hit anything?

Sundance:
Sometimes.

The Boss throws a rock a few yards out.

Boss:
Hit that.

Sundance twirls his pistol and drops it into his holster to draw and fire. The Boss interrupts.

Boss:
(Pedantically) No, no, no. Son, I just want to know, can you shoot?

The Boss removes the pistol from Sundance's holster and holds it out in front of the Kid. He'll have to aim and fire the traditional way. Sundance misses by a foot. The Boss ambles away, underwhelmed. Without looking at him, Sundance quietly asks an important question.

Sundance:
Can I move?

Boss:
Move? What the hell you mean, move?

Sundance quickly drops into his gunfighting crouch, draws, and fires twice like lightning. The first shot hits the rock and sends it up into the air. The second shot hits it in the air and explodes it to pieces.

Sundance:
I'm better when I move.

Note how the overbearing Boss expects to see outstanding results from a PROCESS followed by mediocre shooters. The Sundance Kid is far from a mediocre shooter; he's an unconscious competent. When The Boss forces him to conform to the rigors of standard PROCESS, it destroys his creativity and ability to actually solve the problem in a quick and effective manner, which is a primary requisite of the job at hand.

Turn him loose and, POW! You see things done that nobody else can do. Like the Sundance Kid, a Hired Gun delivers superior results without the Suits' PROCESS or having to think about it. The Hired Gun just gets it done.

3 - You Take Control of Your Own Life

What is the pivot point for determining whether to stay or leave our jobs? How do we know when it's time to make a dramatic change in our lives? How do we make that change? What are the new thoughts we put into our minds to stop-analyze-decide-execute?

> **"It isn't how hard ya hit. It's how hard you can get hit and keep moving forward."**
> *—World Heavyweight Champion Rocky Balboa*

Personally, I've always been a counter-puncher. I have my strategies plus plans for the execution of tactics to achieve them, but what really fires me up is taking a shot I didn't expect and coming back at it. Consider the letter below one of my proudest possessions and succinct evidence of successfully bouncing back from one sales position into another one.

The day I got whacked after five years at a job that would be worth $300,000 a year in 2018, I dropped by a friend's business to take her to lunch. But I missed her. She had taken her entire staff out to "celebrate." When I caught up with them, I learned that my friend and The Boss of her fledgling company's largest account had tangled on the phone for what amounted to the equivalent of a fight lasting 15 three-minute rounds. Unfortunately, this ended with her getting TKO'd. Two million dollars in annual revenue went out the door.

I said I happened to have some time on my hands and volunteered to help her with sales to generate new revenue. (For those who like to say, "There's no job security in sales," it took all of about two hours to be reemployed in a solid position by A Boss.) A few months later, she called me into her office, thanked me for my help, and asked if there was anything she could do as a gesture of appreciation.

I made a small inexpensive request—just a letter from her desk as CEO to the Suit who fired me, thanking him for making me available to help her out. She cc'd it to His Boss, aka The Boss. Here is her letter:

The [redacted] Co.

February 19, [redacted]

Mr. [redacted]
Dallas, TX [redacted]

Dear [redacted]

Thank you for making the services of Robert Workman available by releasing him from the [redacted] sales team. On January 1, I secured him in the free agent draft to become a playmaker for us in the home furnishings industry.

In the past six weeks he has brought back into our fold an account worth two million dollars of annual revenue which we had lost, sold seven other new independent accounts, revamped our customer service department, and is currently closing on two large chains.

Wishing you success in your future.

Sincerely,

Whitney [redacted]
C.E.O.

PS: No, you cannot have him back.

cc: Mr. Carl [redacted]

Dear Whitney,
You are indeed very fortunate to have Bob on your team.
Carl

4 - You Live in Your Child Ego State

Have you ever heard the comment, "Salespeople act like such children!" Did you hear it today? How many times? Well, they're right. We do, for good reason. The correct reply to the comment, "Salespeople act like children!" is, "**Yes, we do!**" followed by three important observations:

First – Kids have fun! I want to have fun! Life is a precious gift, and life is short. I want to open packages when they're delivered to me. I want to laugh. I'm going to make sure I appreciate it and enjoy this one-time-only tour as much as possible.

The inner child of a sales rep says, "Why feel compelled to report to a Boof every day in a suit to manage a bunch of reports and data?" Does that sound like fun for a typical salesperson's Type A personality?

Second – The job of sales is to sell, i.e. to produce revenue for your company. That means helping other people decide to buy. Note the operative words: "People," "Buy," and "Decide." It is undeniable that most people make most of their buying decisions in their *Child ego state.*

This may not be the case if the point of sale is a government lowest bid PROCESS for parts to a NASA space launch.

But if you sell residential homes, cars, boats, clothes, shoes, jewelry, or even software solutions, advertising programs or commercial office leases, try to convince me people don't make buying decisions in their Child ego state, and you'll be arguing a provable fallacy.

In 1964, Dr. Eric Berne wrote the popular book, *Games People Play,* about Transactional Analysis, a psychoanalytic theory where our various ego states are analyzed to understand our behavior in social interactions. The Child ego state comprises one-third of Transactional Analysis (along with the Adult and Parent states) and is the state of mind that says, "That's good. I like that. I want that. Hell, I'm going to pull the trigger and buy that," with the innocence and enthusiasm of a child.

You can perform all the Ben Franklin closes you want, logically show features, advantages, and benefits, and present cost-to-benefit ratio studies, but when it comes to actually Doing the Deal, the most effective way to get the name signed on the bottom line is to appeal to your prospect's inner Child.

To identify with our clients and prospects in this way, to meet them in this well-guarded mental and emotional state, we must be expert at living and operating in that state ourselves.

Third – Don't try to make me feel un-OK about myself because you feel un-OK about yourself. I reject the opinions of anyone who is uncomfortable around positive people and feels the need to bring others down to their level.

The law of negative gravity:

Five positive people can't pull one negative person up, but one negative person can pull five positive people down.

I learned this mode of self-preservation from another excellent reference on Transactional Analysis by Thomas Harris titled, *I'm OK - You're OK*. The book's title describes the best of four human "life positions." These four positions are:

1. I'm Not OK, You're OK
2. I'm Not OK, You're Not OK
3. I'm OK, You're Not OK
4. I'm OK, You're OK

Think about this: Are you OK with yourself, and do you also feel OK around other people? Do you have fun in your job? If "Yes!" is your reply, then you're guilty of acting like a child.

Kids like to have fun, and I bet I know where you experience your professional fun. It's when you work with your clients, not when you get back to the office to work with your higherups, typing reports, spreadsheets, forecasts, projections, and enduring beatings—I mean, meetings.

Your manager or sales admin, or significant other may say, "Why is it OK for you to behave like a child?" What they're really saying is, "How come you get to, but I don't!" Now who's behaving like a child?

At least we know it, admit it, and deal with it. We make it a conscious choice in order to succeed in our jobs. Subconsciously, we may have even entered the sales profession *because* we have fun!

Ab Absurdo

Someone who says, "Salespeople act like children" is employing *ab absurdo.* In their 2000 book, *Critical Thinking,* philosophers, Brooke Noel Moore and Richard Parker, show that *ab absurdo* (or appeal to mockery) is a fraudulent attempt to put forth an opponent's argument as absurd and not worthy of serious consideration. In this case, salespeople are positioned as "the opponent," and the opponent's argument is, *"If enjoying life and having fun is acting like children then yes, we're guilty as charged!"*

This doesn't mean salespeople shirk responsibilities; we aren't actually children and don't do all the things children do. We might indeed act like children, but "acting like a child" is not at all equivalent to "being a child." But that's what the people who say this want you to think.

Acting like a child as an adult merely means we have fun, enjoy life, and are unafraid to try new things for fear of what someone else might think.

Fear of what someone else thinks about us is not something with which we're born. It's a fear we *learned*—as children—from those same people who try to chastise salespeople for acting like children. Here's the reality:

We're born with only two innate fears:
Fear of falling and fear of loud noises.
***All* other fears are learned.**

— Law of the Hired Gun

In an October 2016 article posted online at *CNN Health,* Nadia Kounang writes, " We are born with only two innate fears: the fear of falling and the fear of loud sounds." This observation is borne out by a number of other authorities, including Ari Brown and Denise Fields, coauthors of the parenting book, *Baby 411*.

"Acting like a child" means we live as adults and take charge of life in our Adult ego state, but we are OK enough with ourselves to let our inner Child come out to play, especially in professional settings where it helps get the deal done.

Of course, mature, *mature* adults don't like this mainly because they can't see themselves letting their inner Children out to play and resent those of us who do.

So What Do You Do?

Roll with it.

One of the qualities we loved about Roy the Boy when he was Sales Manager of the Dallas sales team, by head and shoulders the most successful operation in the company, was that he didn't back down when some Home Office Vice President of Paper Clips tried to throw their weight around.

Once, a Home Office VP Suit for our national junk mail company reportedly referred to the Dallas sales team as "that bunch of prima donnas." Before this Suit's next visit to our branch, Roy handed all the sales reps' materials with which to prepare for the sales meeting.

> **prima donna**: *noun* - a vain or undisciplined person who finds it difficult to work under direction or as part of a team.
>
> *www.merriam-webster.com*

When the Home Office Suit walked into our conference room, he was greeted by 20 smiling sales reps wearing red baseball caps that screamed "PRIMA DONNA" in big yellow letters. Months later, the same Suit reportedly referred to us as "that bunch of hot dogs in Dallas." I still have one of the "HOT DOG" ball caps we wore during his next Dallas visit.

Nobody told those guys they can't enjoy their Child ego states, too. The ones who complain are the ones who are jealous because they haven't discovered it's OK for them to have fun.

It isn't really their fault. Often, it's just that nobody ever came along and told them, "Hey, you're responsible for yourself now. You can vote, drink, go to war. It's OK now for you to talk to strangers. It's OK now for you to go where you're not wanted. It's OK to speak before being spoken to. It's OK for you to be seen *and* heard."

And, by the way, you get one guess: Who's the biggest child in most businesses? The Boss.

Let your CFO take the elevator to the 43rd floor to consult with adults in boardrooms about spreadsheets all day long. Suits are good at spreadsheets. I'm not. I just don't relate to confining things into little boxes, and they bore me.

I'm staying near the martini bar on the first floor to celebrate life with The Boss. Let the Suits upstairs impress each other by swapping corporate geek jargon as they sit around a conference table and stare into their laptop screens. I'm partying with The Boss, and I'm light years closer to getting the deal done than they are.

Two Hired Gun Examples:

I'm not crazy about trade shows, and I'm not a guy who lives all year for the company paid trip to Las Vegas to work in a show Boof. Although I've initiated many great business relationships on trade show floors, it just isn't the environment in which I prefer to operate.

But you know the deal. We all play the game: We stand in the Boof trying to attract passersby to sell our wares like we're in a Damascus marketplace in 700 A.D. It hasn't changed all that much.

The Boss of one of my favorite companies employed a sales strategy much different from the norm at the time for working a trade show. I understand that a number of sales teams employ this strategy now, but when we did it, we were known as the only group to be this aggressive.

At the time, standard trade show protocol was to call prospects, and try to get them to come by and see you while you sat around inside your own little 10 x 10 foot plot of carpet-covered concrete.

In contrast, our M.O. was to use our own Boof principally as an anchor position from which to operate as a base of operations. We were each assigned a list of prospective clients, and our sales team attacked the floor to contact as many as we could at *their* Boofs.

We didn't passively sit around in our trade show Boof in hopes that people might register some interest in our services. We went after them. As a matter of fact, we got in trouble if we were seen in our own Boof too much.

(We did manage to get in trouble, but not with Our Boss. At the largest trade show of its kind in the US, run by our direct competition, I watched dumbfounded as the show's security team escorted three guys out the door, including one of our top reps, one of our managers, and our VP of Sales.)

We made absolutely sure not to interfere when the prospects were doing business at their Boofs. But when we caught them unoccupied, we cut the typical sales cycle time down immensely.

This was sheer genius on the part of Our Boss.

When The Boss presented this strategy to me during my hiring interview, I could hardly believe what I was hearing. It made so much sense. It was so simple, so hugely effective. Instead of dreading attending yet another trade show, I could hardly wait.

A few years ago, I was working at a huge national trade show selling our online advertising. I saw everyone on my list and had only one prospect left. I saved this one for last because it was a boat manufacturer and, despite being the global online leader in our business for the previous 10 years, our company had not sold any online advertising to a single boat manufacturer.

It was late in the afternoon and my feet were tired from a couple days of bouncing around 400,000 square feet of the trade show exhibit floor as I walked up on the Boof of my last assigned prospect. Boof is a generous term. I peered through the shadows beneath a stairway overhang to see a fold-out table with one chair and a guy sitting alone, peering at his laptop.

I double checked my prospect list, then introduced myself and asked if he had just a minute. He looked bushed. Tired, distracted, and much more involved with the work on his laptop, he said, "Sure," as he rubbed his eyes. I suppose he welcomed any break at that point.

Halfway through my opening, I noticed his face and his body language were altogether uncomfortable. But I also had the feeling it wasn't about me. He needed something. I found myself suddenly interjecting, "Would you like to just take a break and grab a Coke or something?"

He leaned back and replied with relief, "Oh, that'd be great. I've been sitting here working all day and just realized I haven't eaten anything yet." He gestured to illustrate his solitude. "But I can't just get up and leave very easily," he added, "Diet Coke?"

I walked over to the concession stand, bought a couple of cold drinks, and took them back to the Boof. When I returned, the atmosphere changed to one that made me feel like we were old friends meeting up at the show.

He listened to every word I had to say and said that if what I told him was true, it would solve a number of his biggest problems. It was almost 5:00 p.m., and foot traffic was dying. He closed down his Boof and left with me to visit our own several aisles away.

I introduced him directly to our VP in charge of the division. She showed him all the ways we would make his life easier and much more profitable. He left feeling a hell of a lot better than when I met him, with my promise that in an hour or two we would make up for the meal he missed that day.

That night we lit up downtown Chicago with a big ol' Chicago steak dinner, drinks, 8 Ball in a couple of bars, and a Dixieland band at a jazz club. I don't think we discussed the business at hand more than once; that had been taken care of back on the floor at our Boof in great detail. This was Doing the Deal.

Within three weeks, His Boss signed a multiyear exclusive advertising contract with us, the single biggest deal in my division's four-year history. And his company paid the full contract in hard cash, in advance.

He became an overnight hero. His company's special military and law enforcement boats were very high-ticket items in the neighborhood of $300,000 to $500,000. In the first year of their contract for our services, our new client recouped a return on their advertising investment of more than 120 to 1. Yes, 120 to 1.

Prior to our in-person meeting at the trade show, I had followed standard suggested sales *PROCESS* when I first approached this account. I had:

✓ Studied the company and their website and web presence; check.
✓ Called their corporate office; check.
✓ Spoke with *the right people*; check.
✓ Emailed *the right people*; check.
✓ Followed up with *the right people*; check.

And the result? Nada. ✓

My contact at the show wasn't at all *the right people*.

He was someone I would never have engaged over the phone by calling the company from the outside.

He was someone to whom I never would have sent an email.

He wasn't identified anywhere on their site with marketing or advertising (he was in sales).

His name was not mentioned when I called and asked for *the right people*.

And if we were just another trade show sales team locked within our own Boof, there's no way I ever would have met him.

During our night on the town, I learned His Boss and His Suits had no idea what to do about the logjams bogging down his salespeople. But as the company's top revenue producer, he knew the exact impediments, like the comic book character, *Sgt. Rock of Easy Company,* fighting on the front lines. He immediately appreciated the services we provided and understood how they eliminated almost every obstacle.

We showed him how we would take care of the most distracting, most time-consuming, most detail-oriented administrative part of his marketing to provide solid, hot leads. Our services routinely managed his most involved processes and took away burdensome work with services nobody else could provide.

This freed him to do his truly important tasks. Bada-Bing! The faster he got his company on board with ours, the faster he was able to close new deals, and the faster his company would substantially increase their new revenue stream.

He turned out to be the best contact I could have made because he was the guy in the trenches getting the job done. When he saw the value of our services, he jumped on it. He personally championed us directly to The Big Boss back at HQ and got the deal executed that same month.

Within the first minute of our initial meeting under the staircase, I could tell this was a golden opportunity. The tea leaves were laid out in front of me and all I had to do was read them. I assessed the event, time of day, surroundings, his body language, attitude, and tone of voice. Those are things they don't teach in school, and it was one of those things you can't plan. You have to see it, recognize it, read it, and act on it. Too often, planning and PROCESS lands you in a maze of Suits who cannot or will not make decisions.

Remember the Sundance Kid: *"Can I move?"*

Remember the Hired Gun: *"Would you like to just take a break and grab a Coke or something?"*

You just can't always follow the company prescribed sales PROCESS when it involves big clients or prospects, and especially when you're selling directly to The Boss. You've got to have the freedom and confidence so when the time comes, you can shoot from the hip and **throw that playbook out the window**. That's how big deals are done and how championships are won.

The Big Shootout

> **"Sometimes you have to suck it up and call a number."**
>
> *— Darrell Royal*
> *Legendary Hall of Fame college football coach*

I didn't care much about football when I was in high school. I was a track guy who played trumpet in the marching band. But I was trying to determine where I wanted to go to college, and the tradition of great track teams at the University of Texas had my attention.

I watched the televised Longhorns football games showcasing the new, white-hot Wishbone offense pioneered by Darrell Royal. This unstoppable juggernaut methodically ground out its yardage almost exclusively with its multiple option running game and largely eschewed the forward pass to eat up the game clock with efficiency.

On December 4, 1969, in the last regular season game played during college football's centennial year, Texas took an undefeated season record and #1 ranking into Fayetteville, Arkansas, to face the Razorbacks, also undefeated and ranked #2. The game was billed as "The Big Shootout" and "The Game of the Century."

The two teams were originally scheduled to meet on October 18, but ABC Sports had a hunch that a major event in college football history could take place that year. They made a deal with Arkansas as the home team that moved the date to the last game of the regular season to heighten the hype. Texas helmets featured a football with the number 100, and the game became the crowning moment of that centennial year.

This was truly big time: Evangelist Billy Graham gave the opening prayer. President Nixon arrived for the game via Marine One as the first sitting President to ever attend a college football game other than Army versus Navy. He carried with him a special plaque he would award after the game to the winner and new national champion. ABC had every one of its major sports personalities covering the game for a viewing audience of more than half the TV sets in America (a 52.1 share!).

Texas was favored, but Arkansas was more than ready for Coach Royal and the Wishbone. The Arkansas defense completely shut down the Longhorns' vaunted offense for the first three quarters of the game.

When the fourth quarter opened, Arkansas led 14-0. Texas had the ball, second down with nine yards to go at the Arkansas 42-yard line. Texas quarterback, James Street, dropped back to pass at midfield and had nothing. He called his own number 16 and charged up the field bouncing off tacklers through the nation's top scoring defense. Street was not known for his speed, but his timing and instinct were incredible, and he rushed 42 yards into the end zone.

Coach Royal went for a risky two-point conversion, and James Street delivered again. Arkansas led 14-8 and continued its stranglehold on the Longhorns' Wishbone offense. The back-and-forth struggle continued until finally, with only 4:47 left in the game and the Longhorns sputtering again on their own 43-yard line, Royal made a decision that has become Longhorns yore.

Texas took a time out and, above the deafening crowd roar that forced players and coaches to literally yell directly into each other's ears to be heard, Royal shouted his play call to Street, "Left 53 Veer Pass!"

The Wishbone was a total rushing offense that rarely threw a pass. "I've always felt that three things can happen to you whenever you throw the football, and two of them are bad," Royal recalled in his 1963 football memoir, "You can catch the ball. You can throw it incomplete. Or have it intercepted."

Plus, this particular play was obtuse. Left 53 Veer Pass was a deep pattern pass play to the tight end and wasn't even in the Texas game plan playbook. According to J. Neal Blanton's 1970 book, *Game of the Century: Texas vs. Arkansas,* Street made a special trip back over to the sidelines and asked, "Are you sure 53 Veer *Pass?*"

Royal snapped back, "You're damn right!"

"Yes sir."

Street threw the pass downfield. The Texas tight end was in double coverage but made a dramatic catch over his shoulder, gaining 44 yards to Arkansas' 13. Two plays later, Texas scored then scored the point after touchdown to lead 15 to 14.

"I just thought it was time to swing from the floor," said Royal, according to Jimmy Banks' 1973 book, *The Darrell Royal Story.* **"Every now and then, you have to just play a hunch without using logic or reason."**

Texas won the game, the Southwest Conference Championship, and a trip to play Notre Dame in the 1970 Cotton Bowl, and President Nixon awarded his plaque to Royal and the team in the winners' locker room.

"Damn right, I'm sure!"

5 - You Earn Your Freedom and Confidence in Sales

Freedom and confidence enables sales reps to pull lions out of their hats to land their "Biggest Deal in the History of All Time."

As they say, freedom isn't free. To earn it, you have to pay your dues. When you're in a new position, you work your schedule, you focus on closing deals, and you do whatever it takes to get the job done. When the results of your efforts come in, your confidence increases.

You buy your freedom and build your confidence by producing consistent, outstanding performance over an extended period of time. This is true regardless of the kind of sales operation you're in.

Outside Sales: If you're in outside sales, you have the freedom to spend your day in the field seeing clients. You've earned the freedom to pull over for a cup of coffee, or lunch, or to make a quick drive by at a store for an errand that continually escapes you. You can do these things because you rarely ever do them. You've paid your dues for your professional freedom because you're typically busy closing deals.

You have the freedom to employ your professional judgment. You can terminate a meeting if it's going south. You can get up and walk out the door. This may or may not be prudent for that specific situation, but you *can* do it. You have the freedom to take a day and visit all your clients around Christmas to deliver gifts of appreciation because you've earned it.

Inside Sales: If you're in inside sales, you have the freedom to work at a comfortable desk in a nice office, make your calls, take coffee breaks, take a lunch break, buy stuff online and have it delivered to your office so you don't have to venture out to the store. You have the freedom to operate inside of the comforts of your workplace.

There, you can avoid many of life's unpleasantries: Intense summer heat, frigid winter cold with rain and snow, dry cleaning bills. You have the freedom not to deal throughout your day with traffic jams, construction and accident scenes, your own car trouble, distracted drivers who cause accidents by talking and texting. If you telecommute from home, you don't even have to drive to work.

In either case: You've paid the price and earned the freedom to do deals. If you follow a process, it's your process, molded and shaped by you over time to be maximally effective. You exert the professional discipline to perform administrative, non-selling tasks during non-selling hours.

6 - You Do What Other People Can't Do or Won't Do

When I was hired as the extra "dark horse" on a new team initially designed to be seven reps, I immediately saw the huge opportunity at my feet. I did everything I could think of to maximize my efforts and my use of available selling time. This meant that once a week I stayed up and worked at my home office desk until 3:00 a.m. to write up my sales orders and complete my reports.

I didn't want to waste precious selling time during business hours by using it to do these lower priority tasks. I also went into the office on weekends to clear out distracting administrative impediments. As a result, all I did was sell every day from 8:00 a.m. to 6:00 p.m. with a goal of 12 face-to-face sales appointments each week. That kind of commitment to excellence produces results that purchase your freedom.

7 - You Stay on Top of Your Compensation

The money you make is in inverse proportion to the length of your pay plan description:

1) The shorter and simpler your pay plan description, the more money you make.

2) The longer and more convoluted your pay plan description, the less money you make.

— Law of the Hired Gun

First, I don't mean to paint a picture that the life of a successful Hired Gun is a garden pathway to riches, where we stroll through verdant orchards of trees that bear moneybags free for the picking. We make a lot of money for the jobs we do, but there are also times when we need a job just to pay the costs of living until we saddle up for our next ride on a comet hurtling toward a supernova.

8 - We Should Manage Our Money Better

Because the sales profession is so subject to ups and downs, we as salespeople should be inclined to be prudent, even frugal, with the money we earn. But we are also ill equipped to do this by the very nature of the Child ego state mindset that makes us successful in our jobs.

It is an inherent occupational hazard to live in that fun and capricious state. Unfortunately, it runs counter to the responsible and measured doctrine of our Critical Parent ego state, which plans, saves, eliminates debt, and invests in the future. It really isn't that difficult to do. Earn the money. Pay the bills. Bank the remainder. Then why don't we do it?

It's more fun to buy stuff — with next month's commissions!

The problem lies in the fact that top producers often are not prone to creating and following something as mature and responsible as money management systems. Our inner Child looks out the office window, sees the sun blazing on a beautiful day, and hears the beckoning call of fun. It wants to come out and play! We struggle with the cognitive dissonance of knowing we have a monthly budget while thinking, "But that car is exactly the one I've always wanted."

You figure that you're successful, you earn the money, and you make the cash flow to pay for things you want; you should enjoy the results of your hard, emotionally draining work. Your job status is strong, the revenue stream you produce from your efforts is strong, your company is strong. You feel totally secure in your job. You played your cards, and you won! Why not go ahead and enjoy your winnings?

You argue with yourself: The little angel on one shoulder squares off against the little devil on the other shoulder. The angel says, "Fold that money in half and put it in your pocket." The little devil says, "I know I should bank some money for the future, but I'm young, I'm making plenty o' cash, I've done it by going where mortals fear to tread, doing what everyone in our society is conditioned *not* to do. Even if I blow it all, I've got my health. I've got my attitude. I'll get it all back."

In the end, it comes down to your own set of personal values. I've seen TV reports that show how millennials and Gen-Z members are saving money much better than baby boomers. Why? Their lack of confidence in the future of social security funds for retirement. They're taking it upon themselves, and for that they have my applause.

In my first crash I told you about, I had a comfortable six figures in the bank. But when your income instantly screeches like a car going from 100 to zero, and your monthly overhead is $28,000 in 2018 money, liquid assets go fast.

So yes, your inner Child significantly contributes to your success in your sales job, and it's good to reward the little stinker from time to time. But if we let our Child rule our lives, our entire diet becomes cotton candy, cake, ice cream, Hostess Twinkies and soda pop, and that just isn't a success-sustaining formula.

Listen to your Critical Parent as well. It isn't easy or in the nature of salespeople. It tends to be especially difficult for Hired Guns, but there's a time for Nerf basketball in the office, and there's a time for balancing the checkbook and paying the bills. 'Nuff Said.

9 - You've Conquered Our Top Five Psychological Fears

- **Fear of the unknown**
- **Fear of change**
- **Fear of rejection**
- **Fear of failure**
- **Fear of success**

Let me tell you, there are brave men and women who walk with strength and conviction directly into the face of death and destruction, who have the skills to weaponize a paperclip into a Vulcan machine gun, and who are scared to death of picking up the phone to sell something to someone.

I'm lifelong friends with a guy named Louis who, if there was anyone on the planet you would want in your foxhole, it would be him. We met one night at the bar of Nero's Italian restaurant in Dallas, and I listened with rapt curiosity over my Bourbon and his coffee as he told me about finishing the 150-mile cross-desert and mountain race known as Barstow to Vegas ("The B to V").

I had never ridden a motorcycle but a year later several of us were camped outside of Barstow, California disassembling, cleaning, and reassembling our dirt bikes for the start of the grueling "world's largest hare and hound" race the next morning. (I've competed in two-day decathlons and played three baseball games in one day, but nothing has ever come close to the total body beating I took motorcycling over 150 miles of desert, dried up creek beds, 200-foot hill climbs, and narrow mountain passes that day. Louis finished the race with one flat tire and no—as in, *zero*—brakes.)

Long before I knew him, Louis served three tours in Vietnam. This means he volunteered to go back for his second and third tours as a Long Range Reconnaissance Patrol Leader who scouted miles ahead of his Army platoon into deadly jungles to locate enemy troop positions.

On his days off from a 30-year firefighting career, he works in Dallas' biggest gun store. I dropped by one day to visit but Louis was surrounded by a host of Japanese magazine photographers and writers. When he saw me, Louis came over and told me he couldn't really break away for long. A self-conscious look crossed his face, and he whispered, "They're taking my pictures for their gun magazines in Japan. I don't know why, but the Japanese like the way I look with guns."

This is a guy who fears nothing but a grizzly bear or the IRS. This is a certified, bonafide, battle-tested badass. He got out of sales because he couldn't stand the stress.

I knew a mixed martial arts fighter who did sales by phone at night. He could wrap me up like a pretzel and dribble me across the floor before he slam dunked me into a frying pan, but he was so nervous on his sales calls, his shirts became soaked with sweat.

How do we overcome those top five psychological fears? If we don't, we'll never make it in sales. How did Louis overcome fear of jungle warfare? Education. Training. Practice. Success.

Confidence comes from knowing that you know the material. Confidence arrives when a person becomes a conscious competent. How to become a conscious competent in anything? Education. Training. Practice. Success.

We learn and our learning of new material is supported by training. Then we practice what we've learned over and over again. When we put all of our skills into play through repeated practice, we're successful. And, as Sir Arthur Helps noted in *Realmah* in 1868, "Nothing succeeds like success."

During all my years in sales, I used a script I created and wordsmithed 100 times, and posted next to my phone. I didn't need it. I knew it upside down and backwards in my sleep. But it was there, and

I knew it was there, and that fact alone gave me a high level of confidence. I knew I couldn't fall because I was performing above a net.

Before every speaking engagement, I give my speech at least once, if not twice, to myself between when I wake up and when I take the platform. I need to do this even less than I need to have a script lying around within reach. I internalized the material years ago. It's second nature. But I believe a sales rep's third presentation of the day is usually their best, and I share the same belief about speeches. So I try to get the first two out early...

10 - You're a Lesson in Economics 101

The lesson is simple: Supply and demand. The reason it's lonely at the top is because there aren't many people there! You're in high demand because, like Top Gun Navy pilots in Fallon, Nevada, top gun sales reps are in short supply.

Your value as a top producer is a scarce commodity that merits compensation in proportion to the value of your contributions to your company. The skills you've mastered aren't easy to come by. Your services are highly valued, and you're proud of the money you make and like to enjoy.

We deserve to reap the benefits of jobs that produce our consciously calculated discomfort on a daily basis. How? We create relief by increasing the quality of our personal lifestyles. How do we do that? We buy stuff—nice stuff: Tailored clothes that present us as professionals, nice cars in which we take clients to business lunches or dinners, and we assemble creature comforts we can enjoy after we get beat up on a day of sales calls that didn't go well. We pull up to our comfortable home, jump in the pool, have a drink, and spend quality time with our friends and significant others.

Ahhhhhhh, there's the rub! The audacity to live well! ***How dare you!***

Know that in the eyes of those around you, you may be seen as different, weird, a rebel, flamboyant, flashy, high maintenance, a prima donna, a hot dog, a scammer, a tin man, a huckster, a con artist, a snake oil shyster—the list goes on.

You hear people say things like, "It's easy to be in sales. All salespeople do is travel, take clients out to lunch and dinner, and live on expense accounts." Reply to that with, "Say, we have a position open in sales. Since it's so easy, why don't you give it a try?" Get your stopwatch out and see how fast they break three world records as they run away.

To the naysayers, chastisers, and malcontents, it's painfully obvious that you've broken through a barrier that scares them to death. You don't flaunt anything. You buy a nice car. You drive it. But that's *flashy!*

The mere fact you park your nice new car in the company parking lot is enough to stir the green cauldron of envy in somebody within your company. These feelings make them uncomfortable, mostly with themselves, so they direct them back at you. They're like the little rascals who throw snowballs at the guy wearing an expensive hat. It's called "transference."

In a 2012 article in *Psychology Today*, psychologist Dr. Ryan Howes explained:

What's the problem with transference? Rather than connecting with the person, we're relating to a template, [e.g. You're a *salesperson*] which may be quite different from the flesh and blood in front of us [i.e. Actually, you're a human being]. You're treating Jane Doe like she's your mother, or your grade school rival, or an idealized object of desire, (HG Note: Or she's a child who is unabashed about enjoying life) when she's actually none of the above—she's Jane Doe.

Watch out for those people. It only takes one craven person to plan and plot, and work behind your back to bring you down with carefully planned hidden agendas, politics, and traps. They do it because they can't see themselves living at your level. The only way they can feel good about themselves is to bring you down to theirs.

11 - You Don't Seek Approval or Acceptance from Other People

I'd like to share with you a key motto of self-protection that helped me whenever someone wanted to try to make me feel bad for doing well:

"I'm not here for your approval. I'm not here for your acceptance. And I reject that comment."

A trusted sales rep colleague put it to me this way in an email:

> "Just remember that 90 percent of the people you will meet in your life are/were not worth knowing. Don't get upset, give that a second to sink in. I believe we should always be kind and respectful to all as we travel through life. However, if you are looking to reach your dreams and goals, you have to hang with the proven winners.
>
> Winners have successful habits, they find ways to win, they push problems to the side, they will somehow find a way to make it happen. I have learned that the single most important aspect to success in life is only one thing: do what other people won't do.
>
> Be the first in the office every morning and make the coffee.
> Dress to the next level at your company.
> Study your competition every week.
> Do the best proposals, sweat the details.
> When a big sale comes in, brag on your staff and give them the honor.
> Join your industry's associations and go to their meetings.
> Every three months rewrite your resume and keep it ready.
> Go to seminars in your field.
> Go to all company social functions, have one drink, be the first to leave.
> Being prepared gives command of the meeting.
> Relax, smile, make it look easy.
> Just do what the other guy won't do."

What's the formula for becoming a conscious competent in your industry now and an unconscious competent in the future? It's simple, and it provides a confidence that is indestructible:

Education: My mentor, Joe, taught me to build a secure self-concept. To write it down. And to rewrite it. Constantly. He also taught me how to study the Masters so I could learn how to be a Master myself.

Training: Six days a week, I improved my sales skills one-on-one with one of the best trainers in the nation by making calls that he would personally review with me afterward.

Practice: Every day, I reviewed what I learned and practiced it until I felt confident with the material. Then I jumped on the phone and made sales calls. I convinced prospects to pay their own expenses to come to Dallas, where Joe and I presented opportunities to them.

Success: Because of this education, training, and practice, I achieved success. The more success I achieved, the more confidence came my way. When my confidence grew, my need for acceptance from other people receded.

For example, consider the email below from a friend, former colleague, and consistent top #1 salesman. I worked with him. I know him well. If we tossed a baseball bat in the air and choked up on it to choose teams, I would pick him first. Period. Someone would have to show me a very impressive resume and W2s proving consistent annual incomes around half a million dollars for me to think about any possible change in my #1 pick. He wrote:

> "<u>Never work for any engineer</u>. <u>Period</u>. They can prove their superior intellect all day long, but they don't have any sense of commerce. There's always some Smart Guy that invents a widget and his engineering pals say, 'You should market this!' So, our smart engineer proceeds to hire other lower engineers to make his company. Of course, he feels it's such a marvel (he's so smart) that all they have to do is show it, then sales and dollars will quickly follow.
>
> I have had to save three guys from their ignorance. Engineers selling to engineers is a sad sight to see, totally lost. All three guys thought sales was somehow beneath them, that we were over paid, over sexed, and here to take their money. Besides, it was the perfect engineered product!
>
> I would drag these guys to meetings with prospects. These meetings were with top managers in technology, marketing, accounting, and research, and they would eat up the engineers. All they could mumble is how wonderfully it was engineered. Then they gave me the keys to the company: 'YOU GO SELL IT...*please*!'

> One engineer owner and I quit each other, wasn't going to work...he handed me a check for $5,000. 'Jerry, here's $5K. All I'm asking is that you train one of our Help Desk guys to sell like you do. Surely, you can teach him what you know in a week or two.' I gave him back the check and left. It only proved how little he knew. Oh sure, five years in college to graduate in engineering is worth $500,000. But by comparison, a lifetime 'degree' in selling is only worth $5K. None of these companies exist today."

12 - You Are Anathema to the Suits

Hey, some of my best friends are Suits. I just don't normally work in the same company with them. For example, one of my closest friends is the C-Suit Senior VP of Finance for a major nationally known corporation. Thank God we're friends. We'd kill for each other in personal life, but we'd probably kill each other if we worked together.

One part of his job is to use his actuarial skills to figure out how to screw with the sales reps: Commissions, territories, anything that impacts their compensation. You want to know where your pay plan comes from? It isn't your Sales Suit. Your pay plan comes from the Financial Suit.

A Financial Suit lives a life of little boxes on a spreadsheet. But he's in high demand, too, because his skills help insure that the revenues you bring in are apportioned to keep the business afloat and hopefully profitable.

When he delivers an annual yield of 30 percent net profit in an industry where most companies are lucky if their balance sheets aren't drenched ankle deep in red ink, he's one of the most highly sought-after Hired Guns in the nation. You aren't likely to win the compensation battle against that Incredible Hulk.

He knows, and any Boss or CEO knows, the first priority in business for any company is to improve profitability. The second priority is to improve profitability. The third priority is to improve profitability. They know that if they fail to perform these top three priorities, they don't need to concern themselves with the lesser ones because they probably won't be there to find them out.

But profitability is difficult to sustain or build without the #1 external priority of any business: New clients and new revenue produced by sales. For example, the following is my review of the manner in which salespeople have been compensated for eons versus the *new! improved!* compensation plan for salespeople in my friend's company:

The total, complete, unabridged history of sales compensation: Since the discovery of fire, sales commissions have been based on revenue. When you sell that Persian rug from your caravan for 100 ducats, you keep 10 as compensation. Fair deal? Fair deal. It hasn't changed much over thousands of years, because it works.

But nooooooooo, moosebreath! Hold on just a minute! The Suits figure out that's too easy. It pays salespeople real money based on something easily measured: Revenue, plain and simple. As the company continues to suffer decreased revenues, they want to go down swinging.

The adage that "adversity makes strange bedfellows" is true. Local competitors who used to be mortal enemies merge their common task workflows for operational and economic efficiencies. This way, one of the companies can reduce its overhead by firing more than 200 production staff who provided it with its lifeblood for 20 years.

I had drinks with another one of my Suit friends the other night. "Not a good day. I had to fire a friend of mine," my friend said. "Really a great guy, very sharp, great worker. Orders came down: No questions. Just cut him."

I get it. Times change. Adjustments need to be made. For example, we're only beginning to deal with robotics in the workplace, and the fact that long term, humans will need to learn new and different skills. But when a company gets as desperate to survive as the one above, what can the next step possibly be?

Let's screw the sales reps!

OK, every story in this book is true, except the following one, which is meant to give you a sense of how Suits think about sales rep pay.

Late one afternoon, I attended a function downtown that celebrated the retirement of a federal judge. The affair was held at a toney restaurant on the ground floor of an enormous commercial skyscraper. At one point, I went to the men's room.

The room was empty, but I thought I heard several voices. I opened a small metal fuse box door in the wall. There were no fuses or any electrical apparatus at all. Instead, I had a clear view of a dark-paneled conference room and saw I had stumbled into the executive board meeting of Biggus Business in a Secret Suit Bunker. This is what I heard:

"We gotta quit paying these sales reps so much."

"How can we cut back more than we have already? We reduced their territories and increased their quotas. And we created distractions to their focus like meetings, reports, and daily account reviews."

"Well, what we've got to do is change their compensation structure so they don't make so much money."

"But we've done that a hundred times and they still sell."

"Maybe that's the problem."

"What?"

"They're still selling."

"Hmmmmmmmmmm—I think I see what you mean."

"We're rewarding for the wrong results! If we pay them in direct correlation to the revenue they produce, they produce more revenue."

"Well, how can we compensate them for anything else?"

"How about if we compensate them for PROCESS instead?"

"You mean, it doesn't matter how much money they bring in, we'll control them by not only managing their sales PROCESSES but by compensating them based on those PROCESSES instead of how much revenue they bring in?"

"Hey! That sounds like a real hip new concept for business management! I'll bet it goes global once people find out! We'll be compensating them based on how they're being managed: BY PROCESS!

"Exactly!"

"Go on! Go on!"

"We'll do it by paying them based on their attainment of goals instead of revenue!"

"So, we set behavior-based quotas and pay them based on the percentage of the quotas they hit?"

"There you go!"

"So, if their quota for bathroom breaks per day is five, and they go seven times, they get a bonus?"

"Yes. If they exceed their quota, we'll throw them a bone, like a 2 percent kicker on top of their normal pay."

"But then, if they only go to the can four times in a day, they only hit 80 percent of their quota, so we only pay them 80 percent!"

"I love it! Put that into action! Effective Immediately!"

"Let's go to lunch! Drinks are on me!"

I slammed down the flush handle and registered my editorial comment.

All Seriousness Aside...

Hopefully, that compensation conversation is fictional or occurring only in old, established, dying companies. I can't see an entrepreneur whose fledgling business sorely needs daily revenue using a pay plan of this kind. If that happens, I can assure you that you'll soon see another entry on the docket of the local bankruptcy court: ***Shinda, Inc.***

If you take an alleged sales position in a company with a PROCESS-oriented pay plan, that's your decision, and I certainly don't have anything less than positive to say about anyone taking any sales position, anytime, anywhere. I hope you figure out how to make your pay plan hit the jackpot every single day.

You have to observe the telltale signs of what's going on within your own company. Make your own decisions about your course of actions in your job and life based on what you do and don't want to do.

The New! Improved! NFL

To more clearly understand the ridiculous RESULTS that will follow this PROCESS-oriented pay plan, let's extrapolate this exercise in convolution to a different, more easily understood business like NFL football.

In the records of every pro football game ever played, the team with the most points on the board when time elapses at the end of the game wins the game. But some sabermetrics guru finds ratings decline when there's not enough action on the field between the red zones, so he cooks up a plan to change how games are won.

The final score becomes only one factor used to determine the winner.

The highest final score is now worth only 20 percent of the game's final outcome.

The final score must also be factored with 20 percent values for:

$ Highest point total
☺ Total yards rushing
• Total yards passing
✕ Total defense
• Scoring defense

Ties are broken by comparing the relative numbers of turnovers in the game; the team with the least turnovers wins. If the total number of turnovers is also a tie, the game is won by the team with the most pass interceptions as opposed to fumbles.

When we loved the game, it was simple: "21-17!"

But the *New! Improved!* system morphs into a model of rewards for PROCESS: "*(A = 20 percent) + (B = 20 percent) + (C = 20 percent) + (D = 20 percent) + (E = 20 percent) = the winner!*" At first, fans try to follow games with calculators in their hands. Then someone develops an app for it so instead of waiting 20 minutes for the official determination of the game's outcome, they know in just a few minutes!

(Is this beginning to resemble your *New! Improved!* pay plan? How long does it take you to figure out how much you make each month? Can you do the math in your head or do you need a Sunway TaihuLight supercomputer?)

The football Suits throw a giant party in celebration of this new advancement in the game, while attendance and TV ratings plummet, and the public turns its attention to badminton and field hockey. Five years later, people barely remember what pro heavyweight football used to be.

If you're fortunate to get in at the beginning of your company, your pay plan is probably one sentence long. It simply states something like, "10 percent of all new business sales plus 10 percent of all repeat business from those accounts."

As time goes on, the company grows and the pay plan morphs into more detailed explanations of how you will make less. It grows into an open forum of ins-and-outs, of percentages based on revenue tiers, percentages of quotas attained. It might just as well incorporate the phases of the moon each month.

In this way, PROCESS is not only figuratively recognized more than results, actual take-home compensation is literally determined by PROCESS over RESULTS as well.

I will lay you short odds that within 10 years this business hangs one last shingle outside its door:

死んだ

How Coach Mack Brown Learned from Coaching Legend Darryl Royal:

As head football coach at the University of Texas for 16 years, Mack Brown's record was 206 games played, 158 wins, and 48 losses for a .767 winning percentage (www.sports-reference.com). Coach Brown and the Texas Longhorns put their 20-game win streak on the line against USC with its 36-game win streak in the January 2006 Rose Bowl and won the national championship when they beat USC 41-38 in what many consider the greatest college football game ever played.

Prior to that pinnacle achievement, Mack Brown served as head coach at Tulane University in 1985. There, he learned a big lesson from legendary coach, Darrell Royal, according to Brian Sweany's account in the August 2002 issue of *Texas Monthly*:

> "That winter, a group of consultants evaluated the (Tulane University) program's situation, and Royal happened to be a member of that committee. According to Brown, Royal gave him some candid advice about the school: 'I'd get the hell out of here as fast as I could because you've got no chance,' he said. 'And I would go to a university that has 'the' in front of it, because that's the only way you're going to make it.'"

If you find yourself mired in mediocrity by the Suits in your own outfit, remember what Darrell Royal told Mack Brown: "I'd get the hell out of here as fast as I could because you've got no chance."

When PROCESS overrules results, saddle up and ride out of Dodge.

— Law of the Hired Gun

---

13 - *You Experience Conflict with Authority*

I learned how to navigate the corridors of power in first grade. Why I kept getting sent down the hall to the principal's office was a mystery to me. I thought I was just a kid, doing kid stuff. Fortunately, he was strong but fair, and had the ability to take a step back and understand that.

This was my first experience dealing with A Boss. I was sent there so often we told each other jokes and stories. He even invited me to his home for dinner with his family.

It wasn't long before I learned that if a teacher had it in for me, I could finagle a way to *get* sent to the principal's office. Sometimes my visit gained the added bonus of watching a World Series game together with my pal The Boss on the TV set in his office.

One day during the Olympics, a few of us got inspired and decided to run a foot race around the playground during recess. We ran four laps and finished under the suspicious eyes of our teacher. He beckoned us over to him and asked quietly,

"What did you guys do?"

"What do you mean?" we replied.

"Why are you running laps? Who made you run laps?"

"Nobody, Mr. Elephant. We were running a four-lap race like in the Olympics."

Sent to the principal's office to check our story, I thought to myself, "Don't worry, guys."

If you're a Hired Gun, you may have issues with authority as well.

This may seem ironic at first, considering your ability to get along so well with The Boss. But remember, the biggest child in your company is likely to be The Boss, so The Boss understands.

No, your conflicts with authority most likely occur when a Suit in a position of quasi-authority makes bonehead decisions that hamper your production—or compensation. This might happen when you're required to turn in a fifth report weekly. Or how about your new compensation plan that requires a cryptographer on one hand, a supercomputer on the other, and a soothsayer hovering around overhead to figure out? How does it feel when you determine it pays you less money than the old one?

Or, how does it feel when you've busted your ass for more than a year getting a new account as a steady client to have one of your Suits tell you they're taking it from you?

14 - Don't Tread on Me

Below are three extreme cases when I had to go to the mat to defend myself against sales reps or managers who couldn't close a door, but were only too happy to try to steal accounts from me that I prospected, contacted, sold, and grew over years of hard work. These incidents should not have happened, and I wish they didn't, but they did. I want you to have these as frames of reference, arrows in your quiver if you will, to know how this Hired Gun protected his turf.

I Blast Poacher Numero Uno

Roy and I sat in the smoky Dallas-Fort Worth office of Agent Orange, our Southwest Regional Manager. Though it was a bright and sunny summer day outside, the atmosphere in the office was heavy and dark. Roy was my District Manager, my direct report supervisor, and though we became lifelong friends, this was the only time I've seen fear flash through his eyes.

I was microseconds from lunging across the desk to grab Agent Orange, who had just said, "I need to transfer your Tire Guy account to my new rep we hired to run our newest market. He's local, and it's in his market, and it'll help support him."

"Orange, you asked me to take time and energy away from my job here for a week to go sell into that market to open it up," I said. "I'm measured and evaluated by what I do *here,* but I helped out when you asked me to and went up there to get sales started in that market."

"And we appreciate you doing that," he said.

"You sent three guys up there for a week and I'm the only one who came back with a signed contract for the very first inaugural mailing, plus every mailing since," I said. "My client runs a full market buy with us every month for the past year and that includes us printing his pieces as well for additional revenue. I've called and talked with him about your idea, and he's too busy to deal with a sales rep coming by in person all the time.

"He wants me to call him once a month and basically get his approval to repeat his order," I continued. "One phone call. It costs less than you sending your guy to see him in person, and it keeps the client happy and in our program. And now you want to take $2,500 of the income I earn every month and just hand it over to a new guy because you hired him, and he hasn't sold anything."

I do believe little lightning bolts shot out my eyes and smoke smoldered from my ears. Roy's trained eye sensed my body language and anticipated what was next.

Of course, all this was beneath the notice of Agent Orange's arrogance. He slid into his calm, mature management voice. "Well, you know we're all in this together," he said. "It's time for you to be a team player."

"That's the most asinine thing I've ever heard in my life," I replied. "I'm not going to do it. Let's call right now and get The Boss on the phone and ask him."

Orange had no idea I was going to play The Boss card and looked worried.

"Go on—pick up the phone and call Jack Diamond. If he agrees that a weak-ass thing like that needs to be done, I'll do it." I reached for the phone on his desk. "I'll tell you what. Here, I'll make the call."

I noticed Roy ease back in his chair just a little bit. We played poker together, and he was biting his tongue.

"Well, we don't need to do that," said Agent Orange.

"You bet we don't," I said and slammed the phone down. Without another word, I blew out of his office.

Sammy Hagar's "I Can't Drive 55" blared from my car as I roared back to my office in Dallas. As soon as I came through the door, our receptionist said, "Oh, good. Roy's on the phone and wants to talk to you right away."

If it was Agent Orange, I would have slid the dog-bone phone off my desk and into my trash can. But I'd do anything for Roy and took the call right away at my desk. Roy was in his *I'm serious now* voice. "Get back to work," he said. "I had to use one of my silver bullets with Agent Orange but it's taken care of. You kept your account."

Thank God for Roy. But let me ask you this: At the time, this one account was worth the 2018 equivalent of $2,500/month x 12 months = $30,000/year in personal income. If you have $30,000 in your pocket, and I reach in to take it, what are *you* going to do?

Since then, I've reviewed this incident several times, and each time I came to the same conclusion. Anything less than the ultimate Trump Card would have resulted in my losing the account. I needed to run full speed at the threat and knock it out with a stiff-arm.

Rules of Engagement for The Boss

1) Never escalate a dispute directly to Your Boss.
2) Never, ever escalate a dispute directly to Your Boss.
3) Because you never, ever escalate a dispute directly to Your Boss, and you're the #1 revenue producer, you get away with it. Once.
4) If you escalate an issue to Your Boss and receive a decision, accept it without celebration or contest. Be professional.
5) Thank Your Boss for consideration and decision, and leave.
6) Don't ever ask again.

This was a predatory attack and had to be dispatched quickly. I knew Our Boss respected salespeople, especially the top reps. I didn't know 100 percent what Our Boss would do, but I gambled that Agent Orange wanted to find out less than I did.

All Orange had was a job title, Roy's #1 sales team, and the sales rep Orange personally hired who couldn't sell. I produced numerous new accounts worth many millions of dollars for the company throughout its first four years. Orange was two corporate levels above me, but I was willing to face it off in a showdown. Once.

"You kept your account."

I Blast Poacher Numero Two-Oh

I was sweating it out at home with a 103-degree fever when my phone rang. Roy had succeeded Agent Orange in the position of Regional Manager for the Southwest and called to let me know our company opened a new branch. The new office was located closer to my biggest client.

What that meant was that the Regional Manager of the new branch was trying to steal my account and hand it over to one of his brand new reps as a gift. This was an account that I prospected out of our local newspaper, pitched, visited on site, sold, and developed over a couple of years into a contracted repeat client worth the 2018 equivalent of $300,000 per year to me.

I was out of my head with delirium due to the flu, pretty much down for the count, but I immediately called my client. I apologized for my horrible voice, then informed him of the circumstances.

Fortunately, this conversation came after he and I worked together for two years and developed the most successful national advertising campaign in the history of his company. They only used two national advertisers, MTV and us. He said, "How about if I write a letter to you saying if you aren't our rep, we're pulling completely out of the program? Will that help? I'll have it to you this afternoon."

By the end of that day, his faxed letter on his company's letterhead landed on the desk of Our Boss at our East Coast headquarters. I still have his original letter, framed:

The [redacted] Group

March 23, [redacted]

Mr. Bob Workman
[redacted], Inc.
[redacted] Boulevard East
[redacted], Texas [redacted]

Dear Bob,

Excellent product and service are certainly rather important when one company deals with another. The most important element to making those two achieve excellence however, is the concern and dedication of people.

Since our first meeting you have proven that you care not only about your success but always concern yourself with our success. This attitude has helped take us from a limited [redacted] test in two markets for [redacted] to a varied multi-market program utilizing solo and [redacted] mail for [redacted], [redacted] Records and [redacted].

We feel the growth has only come due to your hard work along with that of the entire Dallas branch staff. Obviously, that hard work and attitude of caring people has led you to deliver excellent service.

Selfishly, we feel that in order for our program to grow with [redacted] we must continue our direct association with you. Thank you for your constant concern and we look forward to a rewarding ongoing relationship.

Kindest regards,

Director, Advertising and Sales Promotion

c: [redacted]

[redacted] International, Inc.

I kept the account.

I Blast Poacher Numero Three-Oh

The brief story below illustrates the background behind another attempted account heist.

One of Roy's tasks as Regional Manager was to grow his region so he targeted a city along the Texas-Mexico border. It had only one major grocery store chain, and they traditionally saturated the market with their weekly newspaper inserts. We needed only one full market player to open the market for sales so Roy and Donneybrook, one of our best A-Team sales reps, teamed up on the account to pull it away from the local newspapers and into our mailboxes.

This looked like another grocery store insert no-brainer deal because we provided three times the coverage of the local newspaper at the same rate, with a number of other strong selling benefits. Nevertheless, the superstar team of Roy and Donneybrook just couldn't get the deal done with the grocer's Marketing Suit.

Within a short time at this incredible sales job, I learned about hidden fears. In other words, when a prospect holds out and doesn't buy after everything you say and do makes total sense, and both sides agree that what you offer is better than what is currently in place, there's a hidden reason. Your job is to find out what it is.

I learned more about the account from Roy and Donneybrook, and it seemed pretty obvious that this case wasn't about anything tangible like money or rates. It was fear, specifically fear of the newspaper's threat that they would not take the grocery store chain's advertising back into their program if the grocer left for ours and then wanted to return.

Before he flew to the border with Donneybrook to call on the Marketing Suit in person, Roy asked me to make the trip as well. I had absolutely zero skin in this game so I asked what my role on the trip would be. Roy said, "I don't know, just a hunch. I want you there." I was scheduled with tasks of my own for a fairly intense week, but this was a request from Roy the Boy. Without hesitation, I moved things around so I could go.

By the time we arrived on our flight, we decided against making a six-legged call on the Marketing Suit prospect because it would have been too much physical presence for this first visit. While Roy and Donneybrook made the appointment, I was happy to stay in my hotel suite where I made scheduled calls to my clients. A few hours later they returned, empty handed and disappointed.

The deal wasn't dead but it just wasn't getting done. They said the Marketing Suit agreed with every reason they gave for getting into the program but still wouldn't pull the trigger and make the move because of his fear of reprisal downstream.

Somewhere in Mexico...

Roy and Donneybrook invited me to join them when they took the Marketing Suit to dinner. As the sun set, lights twinkled across the border, and beckoned us to cross the Rio Grande. We hired a taxi, and the four of us enjoyed a fun evening south of the border in Mexico with a steak dinner, dog races, and pool tables in several bars.

Around midnight, our driver recommended a new destination far removed from the lights of the city. The *cerveza* was cold, the tequila strong, and we traded jokes about ourselves. As we bombed along down the road in the pitch black of a moonless Mexican night, I noticed that our suspension-less cab was kicking up plumes of dust on a desolate dirt road in the middle of nowhere.

My eyes scanned the dark horizon. No lights—anywhere. I asked the driver to pull over and stop. I turned around to the Marketing Suit in the back seat and said, "Hey, I just want to know, are you going to run with us or not? Because it's a long walk back."

Roy nearly soiled his pants. Donneybrook nearly soiled his pants. The Marketing Suit laughed. Then he looked out his window, and his eyes popped so wide I could have parked a pair of Sherman tanks inside his head.

It didn't take long. The only word he said was, "Yes!" pronounced as in, "Of course!"

"Well, good," I said. "I'm so glad we got that out of the way. Let's go have some fun!"

Now for the Main Event...

The very next day was Friday, and they got the contract signed. We were getting ready to catch our flight home when Roy took a person-to-person call in his room from our Dallas branch Customer Service Manager.

It was about a malcontent whom I refused to hire during my previous life as sales manager because I could tell he was definitely not the kind of person I would want in my locker room. He was a disappointed rep with a forced attitude that made me uncomfortable even to be around him, and who couldn't sell a popsicle to a parched man in the desert.

He was hired into a new division and made an overt move to steal a national account from me while I was conveniently away from the office. He claimed to our Customer Service Manager that my account should actually be in the new division and belong to him.

Our Customer Service Manager oversaw all orders before they went into production and immediately called Roy. She said the Thieving Magpie came into her office and demanded that my current sales order (one already under a signed contract with the client) be moved into his name.

This was another of my prize accounts that took a year to sell and more years to develop into a 50,000,000 piece per year contract. It was a client worth what would be an annual income of $250,000 in 2018 and resulted from years of hard work. Again, somebody was trying to steal it from me.

"I pity the fool!"

— Clubber Lang in Rocky III

Roy called a meeting in his office first thing the following Monday. Along with me, our Customer Service Manager and the Thief were there. The Suit in charge of the Thief's new division had flown in from HQ. He placed himself strategically on Roy's office sofa between me and the Thief who shuffled around in an office chair across the room.

Roy opened the session with our Customer Service Manager's narration of the events that occurred while we were both away from the office. She said the Thief came into her office, told her that my account should be his account, and demanded she change the rep ID, despite the fact that everyone in our 6,000-employee company knew the account was mine.

Suddenly, the Thief started sheep-shop-shimmying explanations. Even though he was a weak-ass sales rep who tried to invoke self-pity in every contact I ever had with him, he was still a salesman and he read my face.

"[And] I see Bob over there with *that look* on his face, and I understand that you're upset, Bob," he said. "But I'm just trying to feed my family and pay the bills, and we're supposed to work with accounts that we believe should be sold under our division."

In my very best controlled-rage voice of calm, I said, "Thief, you are a liar, a cheat, and a thief. You can't sell water in the desert so you tried to *steal* my account while I was away from the office on company business. I've worked with them for two years and built that account from zero dollars into one of the flagship accounts of this entire company. What's the matter? Were the grocery store reps still in the office so you couldn't sneak around to steal their accounts behind their backs?"

The Thief's supervisor Suit tried to gloss things over and scrambled to find something, anything, that might neutralize the tension. "Well, we need to make some better recommendations for what kinds of accounts are and aren't subject to our division," he said.

I ignored this lame attempt to diffuse the situation with patronizing double talk and fired a blast across the Suit's bow directly at the Thief.

"Thief, you interviewed with me a year ago when I was sales manager, and I didn't hire you then because I could tell you're the kind of locker room cancer we don't want here. We don't want poachers, and we don't want thieves. You're lucky Roy brought in your Suit because if he wasn't sitting between me and you, I'd [...you really don't want to hear what I said I'd do...]. But I'll tell you what I'm going to do."

I got up and stood in front of the Thief. I leaned down, looked closely into his face, and locked eyes with his. Then I very softly whispered what I promised would happen the next time I ever heard his name mentioned in the same sentence as one of my accounts.

The Home Office Suit sat in frozen silence. His eyes were the size of two big blue saucers. The Thieving Magpie suddenly stank. His hands trembled and sweat appeared on his forehead. His pen clattered when he dropped it to the floor. This was 1985. We didn't even have HR. If we had, I would have taken this Thief aside on my own in a private friendly counseling session.

As it was, the Thief's Suit asked the Thief to leave the meeting. Then he apologized to Roy and me, and said it wouldn't happen again. I replied, "You bet it won't." And it never did.

Take no prisoners.

— Law of the Hired Gun

This is the **Anatomy of a Hired Gun:** You work hard, you work smart, you put in long hours, and you pay your dues. You learn the ins-and-outs of your business and your company. You deliver remarkable results on a consistent basis over an extended period of time. When Your Boss runs into you in the company elevator, he congratulates you on being a top producer for his company.

Then something occurs that resembles one of the three previous scenarios. All three of them happened at just one of the companies where I worked. But as Clubber Lang told Rocky Balboa in the ring, "I've got a lotta more where that came from. I got a lotta more!"

You may have similar experiences. I don't know how you deal with yours but now you know how I dealt with some of mine. Note: I won, 3-0. If I had gone 0 for 3 in those situations, I would have lost the equivalent of $550,000 in 2018 annual personal income. But I went 3 for 3.

"Out here a man takes care of his own problems. "

— John Wayne in
The Man Who Shot Liberty Valence

People will come at you from all sides to steal from you. It's up to you to defend yourself, and in certain cases, you have to go all the way to the mat to get the job done. Do it.

Sales reps will try to poach your territory and your accounts. Suits will try to screw with your sales activity, your territory, and your compensation plan. One day, you'll be such a success that you'll get fired.

So What?

Check out **HiredGun.us** where we've posted the **Hired Gun Playlist** for your on-demand enjoyment. It's a collection of FREE songs for you to access when you're forced to deal with the shenanigans of those around you who seek to control you, squeeze you into a box of conformity, steal from you, undermine your job, and who want you out of there because your excellence makes them feel inadequate.

Anybody can use an emotional boost from time to time, especially high-flying Hired Gun sales reps. Music has the power to imbue us with confidence, inspire us, and pick us up if we're feeling down. Think about college fight songs at football games. I encourage you to give it a listen.

Still, as with any high achiever, your anatomy as a Hired Gun won't let you sit still and rest on the laurels of your success. You want to learn more and learn how to do the deal more, better, faster. Everyone can use a mentor, even high-achieving sales reps. Even you.

Levity Break

The Magnificent Seven (1960)

Just about everyone knows this great film, especially with the recent release of its remake, and I referred to it in the original *HIRED GUN*. In this classic Western, the outlaw, Calvera, and his gang of 30 thieves raids a town of poor Mexican farmers. The farmers decide they've had enough but can't fight for themselves and decide to Hire Guns. Yul Brynner and Steve McQueen are the first two to take the job. They recruit several others, then ride out to talk with Charles Bronson's character, Bernardo O'Reilly. They find him chopping wood in back of a home.

Brynner: Morning. I'm a friend of Harry Luck's. He tells me you're broke.

Bronson: Nah. I'm doing this because I'm an eccentric millionaire.

Brynner: There's a job for six men. Watching over a village, south of the border.

Bronson: How big's the opposition?

Brynner: Thirty guns.

Bronson stops the swing of his ax in mid-air, sets it down. He turns around and faces Yul Brynner for the first time.

Bronson: I admire your notion of fair odds, mister.

Brynner: Harry tells me you faced greater odds in the Travis County War.

Bronson: Well, they paid me $600 for that one.

McQueen: He said you got that Salinas thing cleared up in less than a month.

Bronson: Paid me $800 for that one.

McQueen: You cost a lot.

Bronson: Yeah. (Proudly) I cost a lot.

Brynner: The offer is $20.

Bronson looks around at them incredulously, drops his ax to rest on the ground.
They quietly turn and walk away.

Bronson: $20? Right now, that's a lot.

Brynner: Where can I reach you?

Bronson: Right here.

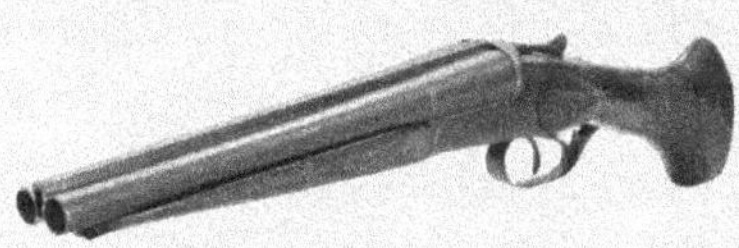

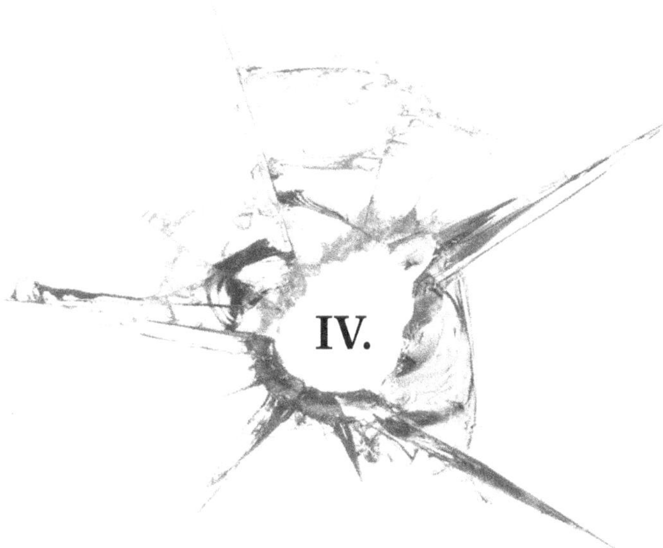

IV.

Choose Your Mentor

In which we compare/contrast the value of coaches versus champions as mentors

---

If you want to be a Master at anything, study the Masters who have gone before you. Learn to do what they did, have the guts to do it—and you will be a Master just like them.

— Law of the Hired Gun with gratitude to Joe Charbonneau

Coaches Versus Champions

Where would any of us be without good coaches? Most athletes would not be anywhere at all in sports without the foundations put into place by coaches. I admire coaches and always will. But when I achieved a decent level of proficiency in my track events, I came into contact with Olympians and world record holders, and learned things even great coaches didn't know.

When I ran for the University of Texas, our track team won the Southwest Conference track championship six years in a row. What took me to a track team as great as UT's was that our high school mile relay team won a silver medal at the Penn Relays and set a state record that stood for 10 years until the event was changed to metric measurements. Also, my time of 18.7 in the 180-yard low hurdles was the fastest in the nation, and my 14.0 in the 120-yard high hurdles was tied for twelfth. Again, no brag, just fact. Because as good as all that sounds, I was still only the sixth best hurdler on my team at UT. Believe me, I've had races where I just flat got smoked.

I was excited beyond belief when I was invited to train and compete with the world-renowned Sports International track team in Washington, DC. Under the coaching of the great Brooks Johnson, I trained and competed with several Olympians from whom I learned things that are unique and intangible. Coaches helped me a helluva lot, and I readily admit I would have been nowhere without them. But champions taught me the fine points and nuances of how to distinguish myself, and outpace competition at the highest level, and how to make that tiny quantum leap between winning and losing.

You learn from champions things you can't learn from anyone else. Nobody else has seen what they've seen, done what they've done, achieved what they've achieved. Only a champion competitor knows what it takes to win at the very highest level, and only a champion can show you the subtle qualities vital to being a champion.

But can the champion transfer that knowledge to you like a coach? That's the question.

Good coaches are conscious competents. They know that they know what needs to be done, and they can share that knowledge willingly and competently.

Champions may or may not be good coaches. They're typically unconscious competents. They know what to do from every explainable angle, and some not so explainable; they know how to do it better than anyone else. But sometimes they can't get those ideas across to someone else. If you find a champion who is willing to coach and is capable of coaching, you've found your own gold mine.

I Luck into the Champion Mentor to Hired Guns

You've got to give, give, give — before you get, get, get. And the more you give, the more you'll get in return. That's law.

— Law of the Hired Gun with gratitude to the late, great Joseph J. Charbonneau

One of the most fortunate days of my life was the day I met Joseph J. Charbonneau.

It was a bright autumn Saturday morning in Dallas, and I was on my way to interview for a job selling ads for a local TV station. At that time, it was not uncommon to pay a headhunting firm to send you on job interviews, and I was about to pay the 2018 equivalent of $3,500 to an "executive recruiter" if I got the job.

Other than knocking on doors as a kid to shovel snow off driveways or sell World's Finest chocolates for band uniforms, I had never sold anything. In my academically minded family, I was told that sales was the absolute last thing anyone would want to do. Their prevailing attitude was kind of like, "Ewwwww—*Sales*? You don't want to get a job in *sales,* do you?" I answered the ad for the TV sales job because I hadn't found a writing gig and needed a job to pay the bills. But Joe's offices were en route, so I pulled in to see him first.

Earlier in the week, I interviewed with Joe's second-in-command for a freelance job writing their new sales training programs. Apparently, my prolific output of mediocre screenplays and short stories impressed him. He asked me to come back Saturday morning. Joe had been traveling but was coming into the office then to catch up on things.

That morning, dressed in a pair of black slacks and a red polo shirt, he came around from behind his desk, and greeted me openly with a huge smile and a firm handshake. We talked about my writing skills, and the job of writing his sales training books and audio tapes.

Then he asked me a question I had never been asked before, "What have you won at?" I was so taken aback I had to ask for clarification. Joe repeated, "What have you won at in your life?"

I had to pause and think.

As I sat across from Joe, my mind ran through a labyrinth of life's events: Academics, athletics, hunting, fishing, target shooting, my happy family life and marriage, the nice home we just purchased, cars. I was searching for an answer.

What had I lost at? What had I lost at? I looked at him across his desk and said with all honesty, "Actually, I don't know how to say this Mr. Charbonneau but I don't think I've ever lost."

When I told him I had another appointment in an hour for a sales job (and about the $3,500 recruiter fee), he said, "I think we can do better than that. Why don't you start writing these sales training programs for me, and you won't have to pay money to get that other job?"

This was not any normal kind of company, job, or mentorship. Joe was just starting to build his dream, an international company that produced and marketed the best personal and professional development programs on the market. My career advanced from writing sales training materials, to asking Joe if I could try selling them, to helping him build the entire international company.

On average, we worked 6½ days a week because it was so exciting. I wrote the learning modules from 10:00 a.m. to 4:00 p.m., drove home, grabbed some dinner, then came back, and got on the phone at 6:00 p.m.

I learned how to work leads from East to West time zones and called prospects at their homes. Even at 10:00 p.m. in Texas, I was talking to someone at only 8:00 p.m. in California. Fortunately, my wife understood this great opportunity, and when I got home late at night, she caught me up on the episodes of *Charlie's Angels* that I missed.

This was my first sales job, and it was a tough one. My job was to convince people to pay their own airfare and other expenses to visit us in Dallas so they could evaluate franchise opportunities to sell and distribute our new training programs.

I was pitching an intangible business opportunity for a new start-up company that meant convincing someone to leave their job, write a check for our franchise, and open their own business selling our new programs, and leading human development seminars and workshops. This required a vast amount of knowledge about human needs and acquisitions that I did not have. But Joe taught me how to understand a person's needs, and learn how they make their acquisitions so they could clearly see how our opportunity met those needs.

What did I get from all that? The friendship and tutelage of my most valuable professional mentor. Five years of intense experience working at the right hand of an exciting entrepreneur, building a new company. A sales education like nothing I could have received anywhere else. An income substantially higher than what my college peers were earning.

Joe taught me everything: How to believe in myself in any circumstance, how to build my self-worth, how to put 100 percent of myself into everything I do, how to prospect, call, and set appointments, make presentations, close deals from the very outset of a meeting, how to shut up and listen to a prospect, lead groups, speak to groups, handle adversity when speaking from a platform, how to relate to people with different needs of power, achievement, or affiliation, how to create gap between ranks in an organization, win success, cope with success, and how to cope with failure. Even how to take a compliment. He taught me Transactional Analysis, Psycho-Cybernetics, Identity/Role Theory, Maslow's Hierarchy of Needs, and how writing crystalizes thinking, human needs, and acquisitions. That's just scratching the surface.

Not only was Joe an incredible salesman, he was nationally known in the business for teaching others how to be incredible salespeople. He was on his way to becoming one of the most sought-after speakers in the nation, and turned down the presidency of the National

Speakers Association twice because he didn't want to detract from his time with his wife, Dawn. (He delivered more than 220 speaking engagements every year.)

One evening, I visited Joe and Dawn at their home, and he showed me his hard-earned designations of CSP and CPAE® (Certified Speaking Professional and Council of Peers Award for Excellence Speakers Hall of Fame) from the National Speakers Association. He had reached the pinnacle of public speaking. At the time, there were only 35 other speakers in the world who had achieved both; President Ronald Reagan was one.

Posthumously, the North Texas chapter of the National Speakers Association established its highest award in his name. From their website:

> "The Joseph J. Charbonneau Award is the highest honor NSA North Texas bestows on its members. It is presented annually to a professional speaker whose accomplishments over the years have reflected outstanding credit, respect, honor, and admiration on NSA and the speaking profession. The award is named after one of NSA North Texas' most loved member, supporter, and mentor, the late Joe Charbonneau whose illustrious career helped guide and inspire many NSA members."

Joe was that rarest combination of skills and talents: A coach who knew all the ins-and-outs of training because he had a track record as a champion in the field. Joe was an expert at stretching people; as soon as I hit a goal, he had another one ready for me. Too young to have planned this mentorship, I was extremely fortunate to stumble upon this opportunity so early in my career.

After I sold in this intense crucible of sales and business development for five years, I felt ready for anything. Joe helped me grow from a college grad writer to a public speaker, seminar leader, author of many training and human development programs, salesperson, and Regional Manager in charge of five thoroughbred, high-level business executives nearly twice my age. I was 29 years old. Truly, after this, any kind of sales job became child's play.

Roy the Boy

In my next step forward, Roy took me from a recruit with a lot of potential to a consistent #1 producing sales rep. Roy taught me to dream big, go after big accounts, and make real money.

Roy taught me not to buy into our company's notion that our newly assembled rag tag sales team was hired to go after the crumbs of the business. Sure, the elite guys were handed gravy accounts that already delivered weekly preprinted circulars in the local newspapers. These prospects jumped at the chance to move into our program for market penetration three times greater with less cost, tighter targeting per store, plus higher impact in mailboxes and with midweek delivery. Virtually every advertiser in our market that used preprinted circulars came on board with us and became their primary accounts.

The elite guys thought they were big time. Then Roy showed me his most recent commission check. He said, "They think they're Big Dogs because they handle big name accounts with big circulations. But they don't get paid anything. Their compensation is their job title. Our commission rate is four times higher than theirs because the pieces we sell are so light and profitable. But they think we're just going to sell little mom and pop stores, and while they're drawing X dollars for 1,000,000 pieces mailed, we make more than four times that amount for the same circulation. You have to adjust your thinking and set your sights higher."

I said, "*A million pieces*? How am I going to sell accounts that mail a million pieces?"

He replied, "Well, for example, I've been trying to get in to see [the world's largest chain of convenience stores] for a while, but now that you're here, their headquarters is in the middle of your territory about a mile from your house. I'm turning that one over to you today. Why don't you see what you can do with it?"

Learning from Roy was like learning how to run the high hurdles from the Olympic gold medal champion in the event. He had been there. He had done that. And he continued to do it every day we worked together. But as great a salesman as Roy was, he was even better as a Branch and later, Regional Manager.

In my humble opinion, he sacrificed too much when he gave up his sales position and took over as Dallas Branch Manager. I was forever grateful that Roy cared enough to show young, aspiring hot-shots how a seasoned veteran got the job done. I also observed how he held Home Office Suits at bay when they tried to screw with his sales team.

One day, I walked into Roy's office as one of the Home Office Suits badgered him about putting Minimum Acceptable Quotas (MAQs) on his sales team.

The Home Office Suit was trying to create something new to justify his job to his higher-ups back at HQ. It didn't matter to him that his need for new paperwork would just provide a new impediment that bled precious selling time away from every rep on the sales team. Roy saw right through this and knew we didn't need any interference from HQ with the well-oiled machine that was producing a 10 to 1 Gross Domestic Product in relation to the rest of the company. Roy replied,

> "We already have a quota. It's called their draw. If they make their draw against commission they keep their job. If they don't, our managers handle it. We don't need to add any new reports."

Laurel and Hardy Bag the Elephant

Our '80s advertising media company initially had two divisions. The alleged elite sales division was paid a small amount of commission for selling no-brainer deals with retail advertisers whose standard ad mix was based on the delivery of high-volume circulars every week in the newspapers. The logic of moving from newspapers into our program was so simple that it made these sure deals. Nevertheless, these guys were initially perceived as the elite group of reps in the company.

On the contrary, our division was paid four times as much for hunting tigers, those not predisposed to this medium at all, and selling them into the program. The elite guys worked with ad agencies and VPs of Marketing. Our team worked with Bosses, decision makers of their own businesses.

A lot of our less than conventional prospects were siding companies, chiropractors, meat men, restaurant chains, dry cleaners, and locally owned businesses. Some others were large companies that were not using our mode of advertising, but mostly because they didn't know about it yet or because they did not use print media at all in their ad mix.

It wasn't long before a competitive mentality naturally developed between the two teams. The elitists had high-profile clients with big names and comfortable expense accounts but actually took home little money. We had low profile clients and made so much money we lived like bootleggers.

The elite guys hung out in their nicely appointed offices in the front section of our 60,000-square-foot warehouse facility. Our guys preferred to office in a pair of old rooms hidden in the far back corner of the building.

Unlike the offices of our colleagues up front, the back of the warehouse was warped with musty fake wood paneling, scratched up wooden gumshoe desks, and hard wooden chairs that could have been plucked from a 1950s city press room.

The elite District Sales Manager once made the mistake of proclaiming himself to be an "Empire Builder" in Roy's presence so forever after our entire team openly referred to him as EB for short. At this point, the manager who hired us had left, and our sales manager was Roy.

One afternoon when several of us from both divisions happened to congregate in our back offices, Roy and I had some fun ribbing EB and a couple of his reps.

It may have been due to the exotic cars that Roy and I parked outside or the chophouse cuts of their discount store suits, but for whatever reason, the subject of our comparative incomes came up. We might have suggested something like the notion that they had cushy jobs with order-taking deals and fat-cat clients.

EB countered with the notion that if it was such an easy job, they'd sell the last chain of grocery stores that just would not pull the trigger to get into our program.

McCartney's grocery retail chain was one account that EB and the elite boys couldn't crack. Different reps were assigned to the account over several years, but they didn't get anywhere with their repeated attempts to move the company out of the newspapers and over to us. It was a comparatively small local chain with its HQ a couple hours away from Dallas, but it was a valuable client and the last chain of grocers not in our program.

EB's guys made up all manner of colored targeted marketing maps with exact prime market radius household counts. They called on the company's marketing VP, the company's advertising manager, the company's ad agency, and several store managers but didn't get anywhere.

Our team was not allowed to call on "preprint" sitting duck clients like this one. We were hired to be tiger hunters and go after accounts that didn't already use print media in the newspapers. Basically, EB's team covered the company's baseline costs with their predictable weekly tabloid clients. Everything we sold on top of that was nearly pure profit. Besides, we didn't want to bother with the reduced commissions paid for mailing the heavier pieces that EB's guys sold.

In truth, EB was fair. He admitted that our guys might taunt them about the McCartney chain being a no-brainer deal but nobody on his team of stars could bring it in. I think I heard myself joke, "Well, EB, it sounds like you've sent in everyone but a salesman."

Roy sniggered. Roy liked to snigger at EB.

"So what, hot shot? You think you can sell it?"

"It's what I live for!" I replied.

EB looked directly at Roy and said, "OK, prima donnas. You guys go get it. You've got a month. I'm telling you right now in front of witnesses, it's all yours for a month. If you get it, you can have it."

One of his other guys said, "Hey, wait. Let's make it a bet. If they sell it, they keep it but what do we get if they don't?"

EB looked at Roy.

I said, "How about a promotion from preprints into our single sheet sales division?"

Later over drinks, Roy grinned and quoted Oliver Hardy, "Well, this is another fine mess you've gotten us into."

Roy already had plenty to do as Sales Manager of our *Hole in the Wall Gang,* but he called some industry contacts to make some avenues into the account. Meanwhile, I employed the subtle tactic for which I was known—a full force frontal attack.

I called to speak with The Boss of McCartney's and got his administrative assistant on the phone. I asked to schedule a brief meeting with The Boss whenever there was an opening on his calendar. When I replied to her question about the purpose of the meeting, she said, "We have a Vice President of Marketing..." I instantly interjected a pattern interrupt to redirect the conversation and embellished just a little bit on our history with the account:

> "Ma'am, please. I mean no disrespect to Mr. Donovan, and certainly not to you, but I've seen Mr. Donovan, and I've seen your advertising manager and your ad agency plus several store GMs, and they all agree your company would do better if you were in our program. But nobody will make that final decision. I just need a few minutes with the real true decision maker. As a matter of fact, if The Boss doesn't agree within 15 minutes, I will terminate the interview myself. That's fair, isn't it?"

Like a pair of school boys on a field trip to a grisly medical museum, Roy and I scanned the surroundings of the lobby at McCartney's East Texas HQ. A prominent collection of animal trophy heads stared down at us from every angle in the room. I grew up in a hunting family, and even to me, it looked like something out of *The Addams Family.*

By now, word had spread to HQ about the account and our bet with EB. Even Our Boss on High chuckled when he mentioned it in a phone call to Roy and asked to keep him posted.

McCartney's Boss's administrative assistant called our numbers, and the two of us went up to bat. But we were swinging from opposite sides of the plate: Roy and I could not have been further apart in our presentation styles.

I worked and preplanned every detail, from my choice of pen and blue-black bold ink to my yellow legal pad, my suit, tie, and shoes. I had considered where to sit in relation to the prospect's desk (to appeal to the right or left sides of the brain) as well as my opening, and the most direct route to questions about their business and pain points. I wanted to present myself as a total professional who instilled confidence in their buying decision.

Roy was just the opposite, the Lieutenant Columbo of sales right down to his signature beige trench coat and rumpled, gray felt cattleman's hat. But Roy was magic. He opened with a joke or a story, identified with something about the prospect: their kids, schools, the colleges they attended, their mutual roots in East Texas.

During this jovial Happy Talk, he slowly rummaged through his disheveled leather pouch and gently shuffled the conversation forward toward the business at hand. Then somehow, sometimes before you even knew why it was happening, the prospect was signing our contract.

Over time, all of us went on sales calls with Roy. We observed the same thing but none of us could figure out his methods. As I said earlier, it was like he lulled them into a trance and slowly closed around them like a Venus flytrap.

So, here I sat with Roy. We had 15 minutes to do what had not been done in the previous 2½ years by several of the elite team members. We would either do the Extra Big Ass Deal across the Extra Big Ass Desk with the Extra Big Ass Boss or go back home and get the Extra Big Ass Horse Laugh from EB and his crew. The top two sales reps in a company of 800 salespeople nationwide went to work—the aspiring hot shot and the laid-back veteran.

It was the single worst sales call I've ever been on in my life. Roy's style and mine didn't mesh. Our mutual timing was all wrong; we disagreed on things. One time, we argued with each other so much The Boss broke out laughing.

It was after dark when we pulled into the offices back in Dallas. We drove straight to our preferred back room because we knew nobody was there in the late afternoon. Roy went in and picked up the phone to call the East Coast Home Office.

"Hi Marci, this is Roy the Boy in Dallas," he said. "I need to talk to The Boss."

We were at the end of a long day after driving a couple hundred miles out to McCartney's HQ and back, not to mention the meeting itself. There was nothing left for us to say to each other while Roy waited on hold for a couple minutes.

"Hello, Boss? Roy the Boy in Dallas. Yes, sir. Yes, we did. Got a signed contract right here. I'll fax it up to you in a minute. They have to give 90 days' notice to get out of their newspaper contracts but they'll start in three months. About 300,000 homes a week."

Roy hung up and grinned. "Ha. I want to make sure he hears it from me first, before EB tries to take credit for it."

Hopefully, Your Boss is adept at hiring excellent people and delegating authority for them to do their jobs. Hopefully, your company hires a sales director who actually knows your industry, knows your business, and contributes to the day-to-day operations of salespeople in the field.

If this is the case—*please, please, please!*—appreciate the great thing you have in your hands.

Human nature is to take for granted things that go consistently well over an extended period of time, and that can lead to creeping complacency. If the above successful scenario sounds like your outfit, appreciate it as a great thing. Don't delude yourself that this is normal, and jobs like yours grow on trees. They don't.

Unfortunately, more often than not, this is not the case, and after a few years you hear the term "Mature Market" bandied about. The new Suit barging in from the outside says, "We're no longer the fledgling start up you guys are used to any more. We have new and increased competition. People know about us and our services like nothing before, and the market has matured. "

You're told things like, "We need to do things differently because of this change in our company's evolving position." You never had to do sales reports or sales forecasts but they become a regular required function of the job. Meetings increase in frequency, duration, and boredom. You make new friends with folks who go by their initials like: MAQ, KPI, SWOT, MBO, RACI (also RAM), EOB, WFH, and WIIFM, and of course, the siblings: Q1, Q2, Q3, and Q4. (I'll add one last commonly seen online business acronym that trumps them all: "404." Basically, ***Shinda***.)

Mickey Spillane

I started my career in the noble profession of sales by writing about it. When I made my first attempt at writing a fiction novel, I put everything I had into it, shaping its concept for months, then taking 30 days off work to jet away to the relaxing solitude of Belize and write. After I had written and rewritten it about 40 times, I saw an ad for the Palm Springs Writers Conference, a great opportunity to meet other authors, writers, publishers, and agents.

I hemmed and hawed about the cost and commitment while I read through the agenda and the backgrounds of the special guest speakers scheduled to be there: Ray Bradbury, Harold Robbins, plus authors of books turned into movies like *Die Hard, To Live and Die in L.A., Beaches,* and many others.

Then I saw one name that made me pull out my wallet. Without another thought, I purchased admission, airfare, and hotel. My favorite writer of all time, Frank Morrison Spillane, was going to be there. My God, I might actually get to meet Mickey Spillane!

In my late teens, I picked up a copy of *I, the Jury* and read it. Then I read it again. And again. Before long, several of my friends read it, and I grinned when I heard them quote lines from the book.

Mickey wrote it in just 19 days. I asked him if he really wrote it in three weeks because he was living in a tent. "*No!*" he exclaimed. Embarrassment rapidly flushed my face. He continued, "I wrote it in three weeks because if I didn't, I *would have been* living in a tent!"

The book sold one million copies its first week and 6.5 million copies total in the US alone. Mickey told me he was sitting in his publisher's office talking about that historic first week of sales when his publisher phoned down to their inventory center and ordered another million books shipped.

They couldn't. The printer made his own decision to disregard the publisher's initial order to print several million copies because such volume was unheard of at the time. Nobody had come close to selling that many books that fast. Instead, he printed only the one million copies that had already sold out. He was fired.

I, The Jury is a relentless story of loyalty, friendship, vengeance, and singleness of purpose with an unswerving dedication to the cause at hand. Whatever it takes to get the job done.

And it was written by a guy, a regular, down-to-earth, American guy who won the Edgar Allen Poe Grand Master Award in 1995, the Oscars of mystery writing. Alice Payne Stewart documented in her 1956 book, *Sixty Years of Best Sellers,* that Mickey wrote seven of the 10 best-selling American fiction titles ever published. He had only written seven books. His books sold over 200 million copies (mostly in the '50s and '60s), more than anyone else in American literature at the time. Mickey was, without doubt, the king of pulp fiction.

Maybe it was because I liked his style; maybe it was because I liked his stories. Maybe it was because he started out as a salesman in Gimbel's Department Store basement in New York City. There were many reasons I was enamored with him, and the chance to possibly meet and "talk writing" with this immortal of American literature was an opportunity I knew I could not pass up.

(Admittedly, Mickey's writing is literature spelled with a lowercase "l." He was quoted as saying, "You can sell a lot more peanuts than caviar," and he told me personally, "Hemingway never liked me because I sold more books than he did.")

When I packed for the trip to Palm Springs, I put several of Mickey's books in my bags in case I actually got to meet him and ask for his autograph. Inside my copy of *I, The Jury* I found a $20 bill. I had no idea why it was there but took it as a fortuitous omen.

At the cocktail reception the first night, there he was! I introduced myself and told him how much I looked forward to the weekend of events. Then I mentioned the $20 inside his book. That night for fun, I used that $20 bill to buy chips at a poker table in Palm Springs. I played one of my best hands ever and ended up winning over $3,000.

Poor Mickey Spillane. (I may be the only person who's ever used that phrase in regard to this literary giant.) I shadowed him the rest of the weekend like he was the Pied Piper. Everywhere he went, I was there. He signed three of my books. A photographer took our photo together, had it developed overnight, and he signed that, too.

At one point in the conference, we sat at a two-top table in the far back of an auditorium while Ray Bradbury spoke.

"You see what I mean about the difference between authors and writers?" Mickey said. "Ray's an author. He has a passion to write about these things; he writes because he loves what he writes about. I'm a writer. I do it for the money. I don't care about reviews and critics. I just care about the royalty checks."

As Bradbury wrapped up his presentation, Mickey looked over at me and tapped my elbow.

"He's also a flake," he said. "Let's get out of here and grab some lunch."

Can you imagine how I felt? I was 42 years old, but I felt like a six-year-old ballplayer who's invited to infield practice with Derek Jeter!

I have no hesitation saying that I learned more about successful writing in one 90-minute lunch with Mickey Spillane than I did in six years of college. Will I ever be a writer like him? *Hell, no.* Will I ever write anything as big as any one of the books he wrote? *Hell, no.* But the moment we finished lunch and he jotted down his home address so I could send him a copy of my book, I ran—*ran*—to my hotel room and wrote down everything I remembered from our lunch until I got writer's cramp.

Rod Milburn

When I ran track as a young man, my hero was a hurdler named Rodney Milburn from Southern University.

In 1971, "Hot Rod" was awarded the Track and Field News Athlete of the Year Award as a college sophomore. I followed him in the papers and on TV when he won Olympic gold in 1972 and tied the world record. Much later, I learned he was attending a *Dallas Times Herald* indoor track meet and speaking at a local event.

After Rodney spoke, I trundled up to him, scrapbook in hand. He watched graciously as I fumbled through it and found the press clippings that showed I tied his Louisiana High School State Composite Record in the low hurdles. I enjoyed a few minutes of conversation with him, and he inscribed that special page in my book.

Unfortunately for me, and fortunately for him, this was long after I hung up my spikes. There wasn't much point in my dogging him around like a lost puppy but his insight was valuable.

It was the year leading up to the 1984 Olympic Games in Los Angeles, and somebody in the audience asked him if he had any thoughts about potential victors. He discussed the names we all knew: previous gold medal winner Willie Davenport, plus the reigning World Champion Greg Foster, and a few others.

Rodney said there was a relative newcomer from Pittsburgh named Roger Kingdom who had caught his eye. He said he saw something in the kid and, though the US was already well represented by Foster and Davenport, Rodney thought he might surprise some people. He was right.

Kingdom won that 1984 Olympic gold medal in the record time

of 13.20. Later, his 1988 Olympic gold medal time set a new record at 12.98. He went on to record the official world record of 12.92 in Zurich, Switzerland and became a five-time US national champion during his career as one of the all-time great high hurdlers.

Rodney knew something that the rest of the world did not. Champions have an experienced eye that can see things others can't possibly see. Even the best high hurdle coach in the world can't tell you what it's like to hit the tape first at the finish line of the Olympic games unless they've done it, too.

So What?

A valuable lesson I learned from Joe is how so many leaders are willing to be of help. Joe used to quip, "Do you know they'll tell you everything they know for a drink?"

A friend of mine in college admired Muhammad Ali, so he wrote a letter to him and asked if he could visit The Greatest at his training camp. Ali invited him up for an entire summer, and he lived at the training camp with The Champ, his trainers, sparring partners, everyone. There's just no value you can possibly put on an experience like that.

Who would you love to learn from?

It's not a mentor's responsibility to mentor, it's the responsibility of the mentee to seek mentorship and appropriate it.

— Josh Hatcher,
"Manlihood: The 12 Pillars of Masculinity"

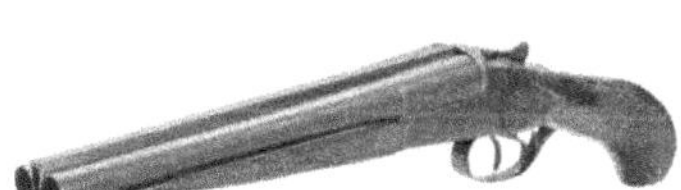

Levity Break

What's a High-Ticket Item?

I was the newest sales rep when I joined a team of case-hardened veterans at an advertising media company in the '80s.

It was a new company based on a new concept, and we were the new sales team. Commando, our sales manager, did a fantastic job of hiring seven excellent sales people, and took me on for his eighth and last available position as an experiment.

A minor power struggle began only three months into our jobs between Commando and EB (the self-proclaimed "Empire Builder"), who were sales managers of two separate and distinct sales divisions.

Commando was a guy with a lot of outside sales experience who didn't play petty parlor politics; Empire Builder came from selling retail. He claimed he had seen the future of the company, and he was there to climb the corporate ladder. This, for a company that hadn't even had time to lean ladders against the wall.

One morning, as Commando led a short sales meeting about some of the things we ran into in the field, EB decided to interject and boast about his importance. EB's stature erred on the side of a Lilliputian. He liked to stroll back and forth and bluster in a voice an octave lower than normal when he addressed a group, kind of like Barney Fife in *The Andy Griffith Show*.

He said, "I didn't want to interrupt your meeting but I saw some new faces in here and thought I'd introduce myself." *Crickets: chirp...chirp...*

EB had taken pains to make himself a key figure in the final job interview for every one of us so it seemed funny that he felt compelled to reintroduce himself. We already knew who he was; we also knew that this was our meeting and that we didn't report to him. But I was just the new kid so I sat quietly next to some guy in his camel raincoat and rumpled old Stetson hat, and listened.

"I'm [the Empire Builder]," EB pontificated. "I sold high-ticket items for Defunct Department Stores in East Jesus Junction, Idaho."

Directly behind me, one of our guys quipped, "Hey EB, what's a high-ticket item at Defunct Department Stores? A $400 washing machine?"

The room broke apart with laughter. Commando had to contain himself, but we didn't…so we didn't.

Truthfully, I don't remember anything else about the meeting, but I'll never forget that moment when I knew I found my team.

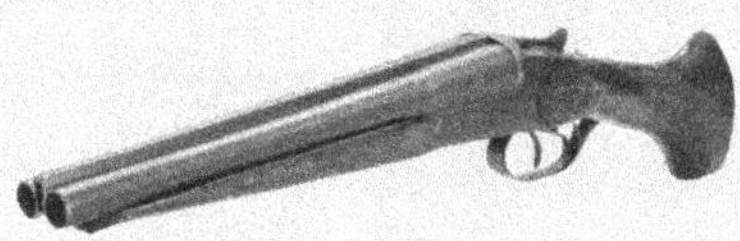

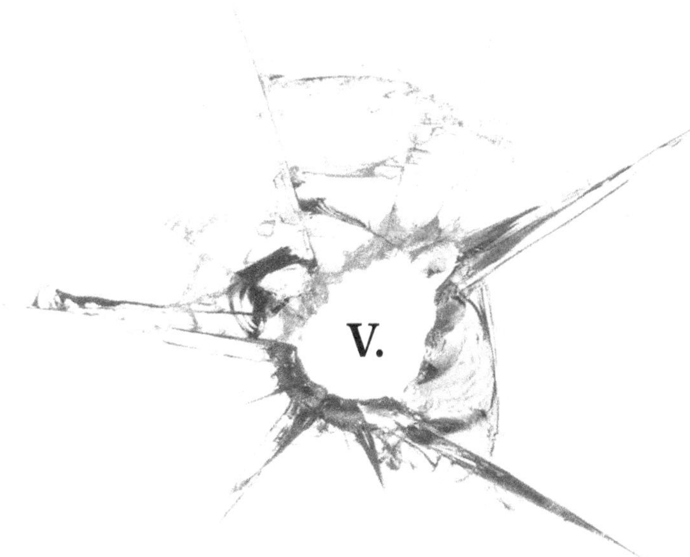

V.

How Businesses Grow, and Die

In which we review five cases of world leading sales organizations; why and how each one began, their explosive growth, and why all but one is Shinda

These are the case histories of my five best sales jobs, how each one began, how each ended, and why.

You will see from my firsthand experience how successful sales gigs have critical common denominators regardless of era, industry, or initial leadership quality. They normally begin with having to overcome a lot of inertia, then gain momentum through company-wide hard work and cooperation, which develops so much forward power it seems that there is no end in sight to progress and growth. But then they get top heavy with management, things get political, business begins to slow, and eventually, they crash and burn.

I've been fortunate to be part of some of the greatest sales teams ever, in my humble opinion, and I've been honored and proud to be part of them. Each and every time I joined one of these groups, I objectively evaluated the other team members and accepted the fact that I was the newest, weakest member. Eventually, through a lot of hard work and some lucky breaks, I became the top revenue producer at each one, maybe for a month, maybe for a quarter, maybe for several years.

When things changed, I left. Then the company was gone. For times like this, my friend and fellow A-Team member, the inimitable Mo Fo Bro, employed the term ***Shinda***—Japanese for death.

The following accounts of my top five sales positions provide an unabashed look inside each innovative, exciting company, and the consistent pattern each one followed: Struck like a match, launched off the ground, torched across the sky like a comet, and blasted into the stratosphere before flaming out and nose-diving to the boulevard of broken dreams. They float around now in the business cosmos of once-great companies like dead stars.

The '70s — The Spoken Word Era — Joseph J. Charbonneau

It all began with Joe, who built one of the most successful insurance agencies in the Midwest. In order to improve himself, he bought and studied whatever personal and professional development programs he could find.

Joe got hooked on the fascinating work of helping people improve their lives, to the extent that he chose this as his own new career direction. He bought a distributorship to sell and implement those self-improvement programs, and won the company's International Distributor of the Year award two years in a row against hundreds of like-minded entrepreneurs.

I first got to know Joe when I was 25. At that young, naive age I found it ironic that the owners of that company, who created and developed the programs Joe sold, would also do things that alienated their top producing distributor. Now, I don't find it surprising at all, having been through similiar events numerous times over the course of my career. As a result, Joe decided to develop and market his own self-improvement programs with improvements over the designs from his previous company.

He and his wife, Dawn, an actuarial genius who worked at one of the Big Four accounting firms, examined US markets and chose Dallas as the most promising place to start a new business. This is where I came in, fresh out of college with two degrees in creative writing.

Joe hired the best researchers to glean information from more than 200 books about sales, sales management, management, human psychology, business theory, and business practices, and he hired talented writers to create his collections of personal and professional improvement programs along with the top vocal talent to record audio texts. He recruited and hired the best salespeople he could find and built a nationwide organization that competed effectively against others in the industry.

During my five-year tour, I migrated from writing many of our programs to selling franchises of the business nationally and internationally, and recruiting Regional Directors who expanded the national operation through their regional offices. I recruited five heavyweights away from their companies to become Regional Directors: A VP of IBM, a VP of Avon, the GM and President of Levi Strauss in Canada, an entrepreneur who owned a shipbuilding company in the southeast, and so on. Joe awarded me the first annual golden eagle trophy for "Top Regional Director," still proudly displayed on my desk.

When the Roaring '80s hit, I saw a big world out there and wanted to ride off to pursue my own dreams. It was without doubt the most difficult and stressful career decision I ever made. The stress of it caused me to lose my lunch. Twice.

Joe gave me his blessing and genuinely wished me the very best. Not too long after that, he sold the company and focused his energy in the direction of his true underlying passion—a dazzling public speaking career.

Unfortunately, without Joe's personal and direct leadership, the other high-achieving champions we recruited drifted away as well. A couple years later, the company we built was gone. Without its original leadership, the company just didn't have the committed initiative and direction to sustain the momentum we created. It happens. *Shinda.*

The '80s — Print Media & Roy

The next chapter in my sales development involved a little direct mail company in the Northeast. A brilliant entrepreneur learned that existing postal regulations permitted mailing out multiple printed advertisements, comingled together in bundles via third-class mail for one very low postage rate.

The Boss seized this opportunity when he obtained a national mailing list created and maintained by the US Postal System that provided 98 percent deliverability to the addresses. Plus, the carriers loved us because this USPS list of addresses (and therefore the mail they received from us) was presorted according to their daily walking route. They often just placed other mail inside our bundles as a convenient delivery vehicle, then slid the whole thing into each mailbox.

When clients moved into our mail program, they printed less and delivered less, yet achieved significant increases in their ad responses due to the heightened penetration of their prime market areas. We provided them with three times the market penetration they got from newspapers, plus we targeted ad deliveries down to specific zip codes around each store location. This refined targeting meant smaller press runs, which created significant client savings on print costs. Newspapers hated us; clients loved us.

Case in Point:

On one of my earliest sales calls for this company, I had an appointment to meet the founder and owner of a large Chrysler-Dodge car dealership in Dallas. I was just 29 years old and brushed some lint from my best new suit as I waited outside his office. Coincidentally, he was occupied in a meeting with a rep from the local major daily newspaper.

I suddenly heard my prospect emit a loud unrestrained groan, followed by the curse of a naval officer whose ship just took a hit. The newspaper was raising its rates again.

I sat across from the gatekeeper and had to suppress a snicker when I heard The Boss chew him out, "Damn it, you guys do this all the time! I wish there was another source for me to get my ads out there because I would take it and run you out of my office!" A couple of minutes later, I walked in, looked him squarely in the eye, shook hands and said, "Hello (Boss). I'm the guy you've been wanting to meet so you can run the newspapers out of your office."

Ten minutes into my promised 15-minute opening presentation, he stopped me and invited me to lunch. Over some delicious Texas BBQ, he chuckled when I told him I just bought my first "ranch." He said, "You call seven acres a ranch?" Then he signed a one-year contract to run with us every month.

Roy's Raiders

For a few short and glorious years in the early '80s, we felt like we had a license to print money. We raided every newspaper client and created a huge number of all-new clients with this exciting new advertising capability. We were one of the best things to hit the US Post Office in decades.

Not only did we make the work of postal carriers easier one day each week but because of the huge influx of revenue from our company's national sales, the postage rate tier for our level of mailing became the only profitable division of the entire post office, other than Express Mail.

This is where I met and befriended Roy.

I thought I was sharp, I thought I was fast. I had five years of practicum and study under the personal mentorship of the best sales trainer in the world. I thought I was hot stuff.

Roy was calm, Roy was cool, Roy was a good ol' boy from East Texas. Roy never gave the impression he thought of himself as anything other than a good guy doing a good job.

I dressed for work in the best suits I could afford.

Roy consistently sported his beige raincoat and cattleman's hat.

I planned every nuance of every sales call so I was completely prepared in advance to lead the meeting and deal with any adversity I could imagine.

Roy ambled in, befriended the prospect, visited for awhile about seemingly *non-sequitur* topics—and wrote up the deal.

In 2018 terms, I'd sell a deal for $60,000. Roy would sell one for $250,000. I'd make $90,000 in a great month. Roy would make $250,000.

Sure, I was fortunate to log a number of large clients into the company's books and consistently rank at the top of the sales charts.

But very truly, I didn't become the #1 guy until Roy took the job as District Sales Manager.

We made calls, sold deals, made more calls, sold more deals, and made more money. On three separate occasions, the revenues created by the Dallas branch alone saved the company from going bankrupt after it had expanded to open new markets and new branch offices too quickly.

On a flight to West Texas after Roy acceded to the position of Regional Manager, I asked him about the Gross National Product of our branch. I was curious to know how much mail our sales team sold into our company's markets outside of Dallas compared to how much mail we took in from all other branch offices, combined.

We did some quick scribbling on a cocktail napkin and determined it was 500 million pieces of mail per year sold out of Dallas into other markets versus only 50 million mailers coming into our market from all outside branches. Our GNP was 10 to 1.

By age 29 the sales skills I learned from Joe, coupled with further in-the-trenches mentorship from Roy, took my brand new little sales territory from no revenue to one which produced more than $5 million a year and paid a pretty nice income.

Eventually, the founder and original Boss sold the company to one of the world's largest ad media companies and hightailed it to Mexico. This put into place a bunch of corporate Suits who wormed their way into positions in the Home Office and worked only to climb the corporate ladder. Their career objectives were to preserve security in their jobs, not by merit but by petty politics.

At one meeting, Roy told the Home Office Suits, "I can't believe our company now has a Vice President of Paper Clips." It was only funny because it was true.

Within three years, Roy increased our Dallas branch's annual net profit to more than $5 million per year from $200,000 when he took over the position. In the process, he made a lot of money.

His ultimate reward came when the new Suits made an unannounced swoop into Dallas on his birthday, the day his three-year, no-cut contract expired, and they fired him. How long do you think the rest of us were going to last?

Within a few years, this successful innovative company sold, then resold. Now it's just another piece of fruit that got digested in the belly of its buyer. *Shinda.*

The '90s — The Satellite TV Era

It all began simply enough when a successful entrepreneur made some time to visit with the man who installed a new residential satellite dish in his backyard.

This Boss owned several car dealerships and was amazed when he learned how satellite TV technology beamed a televised message up to a satellite, where it was downlinked and then could be viewed at other sites anywhere in the continental US via closed circuit satellite dish reception.

(This was 1986. Internet? Nope.)

This Boss considered the expense of bringing an outside speaker or trainer into one of his dealerships for his staff's professional development. It didn't take long for him to determine that he could save thousands of dollars, and provide speakers and trainers to all of his car dealerships at one time by uplinking broadcasts to a satellite and downlinking them via receiving dishes.

This new company videotaped a speaker in one studio location and delivered the telecast to his car dealerships by installing a satellite receiving dish on each roof. Then he had an even better idea: why not sell this same broadcast delivery service to car dealers nationwide?

He recruited his top sales guy from another one of his businesses and sent up a trial balloon to car dealers in the area. He and his top salesman divided their efforts. The Boss visited his colleagues in person in his limo all around Dallas. The salesman contacted as many as he could by telephone. At the end of the first day, The Boss returned, beaming with the success of having sold three dealerships. His salesman, meantime, sold 11.

His first satellite TV network was born, and so was his first sales team of inside sales reps. The Boss's new company provided the very best sales training and motivation speakers to the car dealership clients, then added other training services like accounting and inventory management. Meanwhile, his sales team wrote up deals every day for new car dealerships that signed on to get the telecasts.

I heard about this exciting new company from a salesman who previously worked for me in my own direct mail business. The $15,000 per month he was earning at this new company in the very early '90s is equal to an annual 2018 income of about $345,000 a year. It was pretty difficult for me to recruit him away from that.

At that point, I had built my own little direct mail outfit for three years. But in January 1991, our postage rates doubled the same time that the Persian Gulf War (a.k.a.: Desert Storm) hit. One advertiser after another told me, "I'm just going to wait and see what happens with this new war." I countered with, "What does a war 5,000 miles away overseas have to do with whether a business buys an office desk from you in Dallas, Texas?" To little avail.

With my primary cost of business (postage) doubling at the same time that repeat clients stopped advertising, it was time for me to get another good sales job where I could make a lot of money.

My friend was still doing great with his job selling distance learning via satellite TV, and as we rotated through a batting cage one night, he told me about his company opening a new public safety satellite TV network. They were forming a new sales team. Once again, I was fortunate to gain a spot on a hot new sales team in an exciting, innovative company.

Here's Why I Got Whacked - This Time

Six months later, I was demoted to National Sales Manager of that sales team. While I ran our public safety network's sales team, we closed 11 deals more per month on average than my predecessor, but I got whacked anyway. (This was just part of daily life at this aggressive sales-driven company. Eventually, everybody got whacked. My girlfriend at the time made a mobile of little rubber sharks chasing each other that I hung from the ceiling over my desk.)

Just before this happened, the company bought another closed circuit educational satellite TV network that cost a *lot* of money because it focused on medical- and hospital-oriented educational programs. Not only was the acquisition cost relatively high, so was the cost of production and accreditation for the healthcare market.

Concerned for the financial success of this potentially huge moneymaker, the company plucked the top sales rep from each of its 10 sales teams to assemble one big, bad All-Star sales team for this high-end network. I was cooking along in my well-paid sales manager role, outproducing my predecessor. It would have been difficult to persuade me to leave that lucrative position for a sales Boof in an unknown new network.

But what if I was fired? I could be offered a sales position in any network within the company I selected. And anybody who knows me knows I'm going to take the brand new team with the highest ticket item that pays the biggest commissions. That just happened to be the newly acquired hospital/medical network, and it became my new sales team.

Here We Go Again...

I was in my unmarried single phase, so I got up daily at 5:00 a.m., got to work at 7:00, and worked until 7:00 p.m. I came into the office every other weekend but limited my extracurricular work to just two weekends a month in order to avoid burnout. The work I performed during these extracurricular weekend office sessions became the MO of my ongoing success. I told anyone who asked, "I make my money on weekends."

There was nobody else in our high-rise north Dallas offices because the AC and heat were turned off on weekends. In Dallas, the 107-degree temperatures in the summer meant I went to work on a Saturday or Sunday dressed only in shorts and a T-shirt, and the T-shirt often came off.

Back then in pre-email and pre-WinFaxPro blast-fax software days, faxing was still state-of-the-art, and each sales rep had a personal fax machine on their desk. At the time, most hospital administrators also had a personal fax machine in their offices.

One weekend each month, I jogged from one machine to the next in a rotating loop around our desks and sent hundreds of faxed messages, each one directly to the office fax number of every hospital administrator in my assigned states. This list took me over a year to compile by hand but it was so, so worth it. These fax numbers delivered my carefully written messages directly to The Boss in each facility.

My domestic territory consisted of five states. I refrained from antagonizing my prospects with over saturation and rotated my fax campaigns, only launching to hospitals in one state each month. This was like laying down a barrage of ground fire for total coverage before my targeted efforts over the phones during normal business hours. And every month at least one administrator gave me a call to do a deal after receiving one of my faxes.

My sales included three large corporate groups of stateside hospitals, 100 percent of the hospitals in several states, the US Air Force, plus in my spare time (truly, because I was running out of standard domestic territory in which I could sell) US military hospitals from Guatemala, Cuba, and Spain to Turkey, Germany, and Japan.

The Lunch with The Boss Club

The company rapidly grew with the addition of many other industry-specific satellite TV networks for training and education, and it became the world's largest producer of original television programming—more than ABC, CBS, and NBC combined.

The Boss made a point of keeping himself directly accessible and held a monthly luncheon where the only people permitted to attend were the top reps from each one of our 22 network sales teams. Immediately upon returning to the office after each one of these exclusive confabs, you could bet that every sales rep's manager waited while he tapped one foot and looked at his watch before he implored, "What went on in there today? Anything I need to know about?"

Whenever I got to join The Boss for lunch club, I liked to sit as close as possible to him to learn as much as I could about leaders at the top. For example, I observed he often scribbled notes in a small pocket-sized notebook about things reps told him. Sometimes they sparked him to take immediate action.

On one memorable occasion, a rep spoke with the conviction of Popeye's "Enough's enough, and enough's too much." Across a bowl of bread rolls, he provided specific details about how certain departments were consistently screwing up and documented how it hurt sales in his division (and consequently, in all divisions across the board).

The Boss penned a notation, excused himself for a moment, and walked to the nearby wall phone in the luncheon room. He spoke a few words into the receiver, then returned for the rest of the luncheon and discussion.

It was late December, and our offices were in a shopping complex. On our walk back to work, The Boss took us all Christmas shopping for charitable gifts. We picked out anything we wanted to put in the company's big Toys for Tots box; we just put it on his tab. We were all in happy holiday moods with our shopping bags and holiday cheer when the elevator doors opened to let us out on our office floor.

Oh—My —God. We had forgotten about The Boss's succinct phone call back in the luncheon room. Obviously, his message already was in effect. The scene resembled the ad I used to see on airport walls with men and women in an office setting, all running in different directions as panic strained their features, and flames shot up off their asses.

That was the highest pressured sales environment in which I've ever been involved. I also rank it easily in my top five best sales organizations and groups of sales reps and support staff I've ever known, maybe as high as the #2 slot.

Plus, each month the top producer in each of a dozen different network sales teams got unlimited use of a brand new Cadillac the following month. Our hospital network selected a doctor-black Sedan De Ville, and I was fortunate enough to enjoy its use for most of the year.

As with most successful companies, the drive was there from the outset to build, and grow, and expand. And expand it did, but a few years later when the company's Initial Price Offering came out on the New York Stock Exchange, I should have known to begin my job search.

The clearance sale Suits flooded in, and we soon witnessed the total elimination of sales incentives we could offer to close deals with corporate groups or other mega-revenue producing prospects. But we had lots of spreadsheets! Soon we also had mucho projections, mucho mucho reports, and mucho mucho mucho meetings. These were useful to some extent. They clearly documented the falling sales like an index of the 1929 stock market.

Sales became bogged down by the quagmire of Suits. These guys were so anxious to justify their jobs and appease investors that we found ourselves fighting sales wars with one arm tied behind our backs and both legs in shackles. Then the overall top revenue producer for three years in a row (me) got whacked. A couple months later the #2 rep was whacked, then the #3, #4, and so on.

Within a year of my departure, the company sold. Then it sold again, but the Suits in charge hadn't built the company. They didn't run it with any passionate commitment other than to draw their paychecks and play golf on Tuesdays.

They didn't know beans about how to run it on any level that didn't involve a spreadsheet, and this once glorious company died. A huge free-standing building complex sat empty and alone like a ghost ship on the high seas. *Shinda.*

The New Millennium — The DVD Era

Once Upon a Time in the West, a little band of outlaws started a company under the direction of another brilliant entrepreneur. All of us worked together at the previously described satellite TV company, and we knew from years of successful experience exactly how to Do the Deal. This was our own little All-Star team of Hired Guns.

This Boss had the foresight and temerity to open up shop in the depths of a horrible economic climate, the early Oughts. At the time, the *Wall Street Journal* ran an article about the new hot job in Silicon Valley—car repossession. So many dot-com companies went bust after their burn rates exceeded their rounds of vulture capitalist financing, the CEOs lost their houses and cars, and the running joke was, "What do you say to a Silicon Valley dot-com CEO? Thank him for delivering the pizza and give him his tip."

Our Boss pioneered the concept of delivering state-of-the-art clinical education programs for cosmetic dentists on DVDs. Our prime target market was the alumni of the most highly regarded dental training institutes in the world, and the content and production quality we produced was the very best they'd ever seen.

When we started our little company, there was really no way for dentists to get an extreme close-up look at an actual in-the-mouth cosmetic procedure on a live patient, even if they were in a hands-on classroom setting. Plus, it cost them about $25,000 to attend a three- or four-day symposium to learn how to do one of these highly specialized procedures.

Dentists nationwide jumped at the opportunity to watch our bleeding edge programs in their own offices on DVDs. The training was of superior quality, delivered by world-leading authorities, and a small fraction of the cost of shutting down their practice and incurring the costs of travel, lodging, and meals to attend off-site presentations.

Once again, it was a license to print money. And this time there was no HR department to impose politically correct ridiculousness. As he walked through the sales floor and overheard off-color banter among the reps, our founder and Boss used to joke, "Oh boy! I wish I didn't hear that—I might have to report you to HR! Oh, wait, I *am* HR!"

HR? Not here.

In most cases, it's only a matter of time until the Corporate Geek Suits come in with enticing plans to expand the business by borrowing a ton of new capital investiture and ruining things. Before this happens, it's a matter of who's running the show and how they want to run it.

Our cash flow was so outrageously strong, outside capital was the last thing from our minds. Plus, we were fortunate to have one of us as The Boss, the brilliant innovator and leader of this self-proclaimed "little band of outlaws."

A few years into our company, we added cosmetic surgery clinical education DVD programs with their brand of state-of-the-art live patient procedures performed by world-leading cosmetic surgeons. Our strategic partner in this new division of the company was Johns Hopkins University, consistently the leading medical school in the nation.

We looked forward to going in every day because 1) it was fun, 2) we were fun, and 3) our clients were highly educated, fun people who loved every single thing about what we did, how it was delivered to them, and most important, what it did for them. The fact that it was immensely profitable, and we were all making plenty o' cash, was almost a bonus. Almost.

We had one sales report, the only one that matters: A 4' x 8' erasable white board on the wall behind my desk that showed how many deals each one of us signed during each month. And no matter how hard I worked, or any of us worked, out of our total of seven magnificent sales reps, you could throw a blanket over the finish line of any month to determine who actually won with the most deals.

There's no need for new investors or projections or reports or forecasts when your sales and collective revenue are so great it outstrips what anybody thinks you can sell, month over month, year over year.

This was the single longest tenure—more than six years—I've ever had at a sales job. Six exciting, growth- and success-oriented fun years.

I was at my desk at 7:00 a.m. every day to get on the phone and fax machine (yes, fax machines were still the best way to market to this audience in the Oughts!). As I did in my previous position at the distance learning satellite TV company, I also went into the office two weekends each month and left voicemail messages for all 150 of my biweekly assigned prospects.

We might still be selling there if not for the Great Recession of 2009, the worst recession in US history since 1929. When the economy crashed and nobody had any money, the first things people cut back on were their aesthetic needs like elective cosmetic dentistry and elective cosmetic surgery procedures.

When patients don't pay for elective procedures, and dentists and doctors don't make money, they can't buy clinical education DVD programs. So even with this incredible money machine with everything in the world going for it, outside circumstances forced the company to close. ***Shinda.***

The Teens — The Online Era:

After that, I met with a brilliant entrepreneur from San Francisco but this isn't going to go where you probably think it's going.

This entrepreneur's company is still growing and will continue to grow. I hope it stays open forever, and I never have to add that final fatal footnote of *Shinda*. It's a collection of people with incredible talents and skills delivering ongoing educational and training programs focused on every segment of our nation's public safety community, much like our company in the '90s. But now, it's delivered via internet instead of the old satellite TV model or by shipments of DVDs.

Because of these industry-specific news, information, and training services offered online, police, fire, EMS, military, corrections, and local government agencies pay far less than they've been paying for programs that are much better than they've ever seen. Plus, online technology provides increased access to the programs from any kind of mobile device with internet access, significantly broadening the scope of delivery to a true global scale.

This company has the benefit of one of the most highly intelligent Bosses I've known, driven by a passion not to sell out but to stay at the helm well into its second decade, and to continue building the company with exceptional year-over-year increases in each vertical website. This is evidenced by the fact that he launched the company in 1999, and made the tough decisions and executed innovative business practices to stave off the Bay Area wolves that ate so many companies in the dot-com bust of the early Oughts.

He scaled back, then regrouped and rebuilt to develop an even more robust company with innovative and aggressive strategies and tactics and, most important of all, people. Further, he weathered the following economic meltdown of 2009, continued to grow his business, and emerged as the global online leader in each of those public safety verticals mentioned above. Believe me, that is no small feat; indeed, it's a truly remarkable one.

I was excited and fortunate to join the outfit just before the early teens. I'm pretty good at reading people and knew from my first face-to-face meeting with this leader that he was someone who knew what he was about and where he was going. I could tell in the first 10 minutes of our meeting that this was someone with whom I was glad to throw my hat in the ring. He was confident, reasoned, and knowledgeable about many aspects of business beyond my scope of experience—and also a lot younger.

I enjoyed every moment of my five-year tour of duty there and departing this company was the second-most difficult career decision I've made and executed, next to flying off from my eagle's nest mentorship with Joe. But the time in my life arrived to pivot and focus my energy on helping the group of professionals like you whom I care most about through books, speeches, and videos.

Please remember, these are my five *best* sales jobs. I've had about 10 more but I won't bore you. Some were good places but I made little money; some were horrible places and I made good money. Some were places I made decent money but not enough for the shenanigans involved.

So What?

So how did I weather all these storms in sales?

During my first towering crash in the '80s, I had dinner with a friend who wanted to be filled in on everything that happened. After I relived the agony of those losses, she asked, "How do you handle it so well?" Before I even knew what I was saying, I heard myself asking, "What's the alternative?"

I've reflected on that conversation a lot over the years. How was I so quick with such a confident response? What did that tell me?

It told me that when you write down your beliefs and internalize how they align with your ethics, morals, values, desires, ambitions, abilities, strengths, and weaknesses—when you clearly identify who you are to yourself—nobody can ever take that away from you. You can lose everything else but if you have that, it's only a matter of time until you get everything else back.

Until you establish and write your own identity, you won't understand. Once you've done it, you'll understand and appreciate *Your Single Greatest Asset* (read on for that chapter): You.

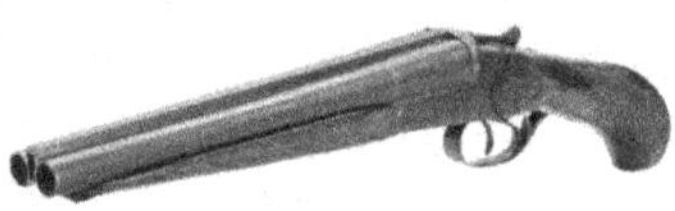

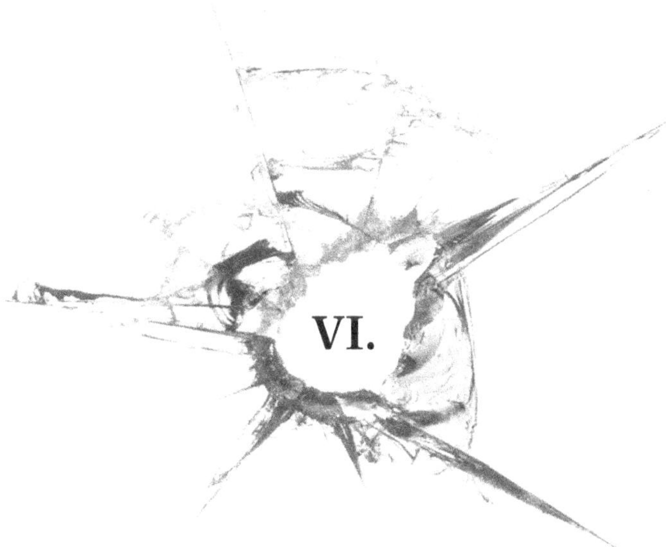

VI.

Growth of the Corporate Beast

In which we examine the general stages of a typical new company, identify when and for how long sales reigns supreme, how growth leads to disconnects with the sales team, and how to know if it's happening to you.

Genesis

The evolution of a business almost always arises from an entrepreneur's innovation combined with passion and funding. Maybe the founder puts up all the money to get started. Sometimes it's investor financing but hopefully it isn't from a group of vulture capitalists.

Now, before I body slam the evil people in the business of financial capital investiture, I have to qualify that there are, like anything else, good capital growth companies led by good people. Just not the evil, wicked, mean, and nasty monsters addressed here.

A Word About Vulture Capitalists

Vulture capitalists fund your company, support its growth, and tell you lots of nice things about how great you're doing, and how happy they are to have the opportunity to be involved in such an exciting operation. When your company generates a respectably consistent cash flow, your leaders begin retiring the debt to the vultures.

Your leaders also invest some of those winnings into company improvements. You get some newer equipment or furniture that is a slight upgrade from the sawhorses and discarded wooden doors you used for desks and tables when the company started out.

Suddenly, the vultures become financial efficiency experts and critique the improvements—they cost money! The Boss gets a note from the head vulture, "This isn't GM!" (Yes, I actually read that one on Roy's desk.)

Before long, the vultures sell you out to the highest bidder, pocket their profits on the deal, and your leaders are out the door with yesterday's coffee grounds. Meanwhile, a flood of new guys pours in who don't know beans about the business. And you're supposed to "remain loyal" and work in that new environment.

Despite all the religious vows you make together, vulture capitalists are not there to partner with your company. They are not there to fund it for its kickoff, then support it during its growth and enjoy the long-term profit arrangements.

That's what they like to tell you; that's what they want you to believe.

Vulture capitalists are there to make a buck. Period. The bigger the buck they can make, and the faster they can make it, is their stock in trade. Is this a knock-on vulture capitalists? Not really. They aren't hiding anything. They blatantly place everything right there in front of us to see.

Look at the exact words they use to describe their business: "Venture" and "Capital." That should tell you everything you need to know. Their business is providing capital to launch hopefully profitable ventures.

The misconception is that the business "venture" in question is yours. It isn't. It's theirs. The "venture" in "venture capital" means *their* attempt to make money by loaning some to your outfit, then recouping their original investment in your company, plus profits. How?

1) They perform due diligence on your fledgling outfit's business plan.
2) They provide initial funding to help launch your company.
3) They keep tabs on its growth and development disguised as "guidance" by placing their own *Mole* in your midst as a shared employee.
4) They observe their *Mole's* reports on your company's pitfalls, progress, and profitability.
5) They sell your company to the highest bidder that makes the first good offer.

Consider this: What is the split of stock percentages between Your Boss and partners versus the vulture capitalists? Typically, the vultures hold 51-60 percent while your execs have 40-49 percent. BUT the vultures always make sure they also hold 100 percent of the Preferred Stock or Prior Preferred Stock.

This means they can railroad your company's officers by voting all their Prior Preferred Stock positions over your guys' meager holdings of 40-49 percent of the "common stock." Yep.

So be advised: Statements like, "We're in this for the long haul," or "We like you guys. Let us know anything you need," or "This is going to be exciting for all of us!" may sound great when your two companies get engaged. A general feeling of optimism is natural in the blush of a flourishing new relationship.

But give that marriage a year or two, especially if you're aggressively retiring the debt back to the vultures ahead of schedule. You will find your company's marriage partner is suddenly single again, looking for suitors with deep pockets. Then one day, your trusted partner who claims to be "in this for the long haul" informs you there's a new horse kicking in your stall.

You see, they don't like it if you retire the debt early because your business is wildly successful. That would retire the debt to them before they have the opportunity to sell your company for many times what they'll make on the mere interest of your planned payment schedule from their initial loan for start-up capital.

How do I know this? The same way I know everything else in this book—been there, done that.

When we opened the super-aggressive direct mail company after our old company unceremoniously rewarded Roy for his loyalty by whacking him, we climbed into bed with a VC firm in Dallas. Roy was CEO, our VP of Production was Uy, by far the best production manager in our old company, and I was VP of Sales.

Our sales were so strong right out of the chute when we opened, we were already in the process of aggressively retiring our debt to the VCs ahead of schedule. You'd think they would like that. Nope. It turns out they wanted to sell us and turn a quick, big profit all along.

The VCs installed their Mole as our company's financial officer—their employee but on our payroll. We were aware of this. What we were not aware of was that the consultant we brought in to help us fight this sellout threat also turned out to be a Spy for the VCs. We learned this too late, after he sat in on every strategic meeting and reported our moves back to the vultures.

For example, when the sellout threat manifested itself and Roy and Uy worked to flush out financing to buy out our VCs, I decided to fight power with power. I set a meeting with a friend who was one of the biggest financiers in Texas and served as chairman of the Board of Regents for a major university in Texas. While I sat with my friend in his lavish downtown luxury suite, we made a conference call to Roy, Uy, and the Spy back at our offices.

My friend called a couple of his cronies to start assembling money to buy out the VCs but it didn't work. When the Spy ratted us out back to the vultures, they sped everything up and rammed the votes through to get the deal done. Net effect: The 2018 equivalent of $14,000,000 to the VCs, and 120 of our people out of jobs.

What had we heard all along? "We're in this for the long haul." "We like you guys. Let us know anything you need." "This is going to be exciting for all of us!" What did we get? Sold out.

Even though we produced consistently growing revenues our first year of what would amount to $35 million in 2018, they sold us out to our old company before that first year ended. Roy and Uy had seats on the board and voted against the takeover. But the VCs still had 60 percent of the stock, and also pressed the vote by invoking their Preferred Stock voting privileges. We were sunk.

If your company is in debt to a bunch of vulture capitalists, make as much as you can, as fast as you can, as long as you can, and be ready to move to another job at any moment when they sell you out.

Point of Differentiation

It's important to understand the difference between Vulture Capitalists and Private Equity Firms:

> "Private equity firms mostly buy mature companies that are already established. The companies may be deteriorating or not making the profits they should be due to inefficiency. Private equity firms buy these companies and streamline operations to increase revenues. Venture capital firms, on the other hand, mostly invest in start-ups with high growth potential."
>
> **Investopedia online.**

In September 2007, the *Harvard Business Review* published "The Strategic Secret of Private Equity," an article by experts, Felix Barber and Michael Gould. They wrote:

> "Private equity. The very term continues to evoke admiration, envy, and—in the hearts of many public company CEOs—fear.
>
> ...the fundamental reason behind private equity's growth and high rates of return is something that has received little attention, perhaps because it's so obvious: The firm's standard practice of buying businesses and then, after steering them through a transition of rapid performance improvement, selling them. That strate-

gy, which embodies a combination of business and investment-portfolio management, is at the core of private equity's success...

...the strategy is ideally suited when, in order to realize a one-time, short-to-medium term, value-creation opportunity, buyers must take outright ownership and control.

...once the changes necessary to achieve the uplift in value have been made—usually over a period of two to six years—it makes sense for the owner to sell the business and move on to new opportunities."

Private equity firms typically own a company for about five years before selling their investment for profit.

— Law of the Hired Gun

<u>HG NOTE:</u> This can actually be great for sales, short term. It depends which side of the deal you're on. This is clearly stated in the *Harvard Business Review* article ("after steering them through a transition of rapid performance improvement") and in the *Investopedia* online definition ("streamline operations to increase revenues"). What do they mean by "rapid performance improvement" and "increase revenues?" Boost those sales—sell! Sell!! SELL!!!

In *REVENGE of the HIRED GUN*, this book's sequel, a chapter called *Murderer's Row II* features our first non-salesperson interview with a financial Suit. These short excerpts from that interview give you an inside look from a financial Suit's perspective of exactly what happens when a private equity firm buys your company.

HG: So, you work with finance budgets, inventory, production, sales, operations, administration, management...you're pretty much the midsection of that whole company, where all the arms and legs come back to that one central point for organization into the overall structure.

CASEY: Right. We had a large outside company come in and buy our company, and they wanted to expand operations beyond our indoor products into the outdoor market. So, they acquired a company in Canada and hired me on to learn the business of the new company they just acquired.

They sent me up to the Canadian company ostensibly to close it down. When the acquisition was made the people up there were told not to worry about it, "Nothing is going to change."

HG: So, the word was, "Everything is going to stay the way it is, we're just buying the company to increase our book value..."

CASEY: Right. That's what they told the original owner of the company, and all the employees. They told me, "We're going to try to work with them," and I could tell that's not what they were trying to do.

HG: So, you were picking up telltale vibes that said, "I know I'm hearing this, but it doesn't look right. Something I'm seeing is not matching up with what I'm hearing."

CASEY: Here's the main thing that really tipped me off that something was going on. Here I was, newly hired into the company, and I had nothing to do. The whole point of me being hired was to work on the project of this outdoor company's acquisition, but they didn't want me going up there on the trips with the execs because it might tip the Canadians off that something was going on.

There was no plan, no real projected thought process. It was just, "We need to be secretive, just go up there and learn everything you can." They finally let the employees up there in on it and gave each person the date that they'd be leaving.

The Good News Is...

Cash flow cures all ills.

— Law of the Hired Gun

Even if you're initially shackled to a vulture capital group, or if your company has just been acquired and newly relaunched by a private equity firm, the Genesis period of a new business provides the salad days for sales reps. Because of your group's high belief factor in Your Boss's conviction and innovation, because of the passionate commitment by all to pull together in the common cause of onward and upward sales and revenue, because the prevailing mentality is, "All for one and one for all" (with apologies to Alexandre Dumas):

You sell a lot.

You earn a lot.

Your leaders are happy.

The Boss participates in high ticket sales calls and proves to be the top sales rep in your outfit.

Everyone in the company loves the sales team because everybody operates so close to ground level, they know that you all have to pull together to survive. As a result, you love your job. It's fun to work in an environment where The Boss walks through the sales floor with a roll of C-notes and posts 10 of them as $100 spiffs on the next 10 deals that come through the door.

You can't wait to get up the next morning to go at it some more. You work harder than ever but it doesn't feel like work. It feels like achievement. It feels like winning. And winning you are—against your competition and against the inertia that many new businesses have difficulty overcoming to stay the course toward success.

In the many companies where I've worked, the Genesis phase normally spans the first one to three years of the business.

Monarchy

After the first couple years of a new company, sales is king. Your company grows because of the steady stream of revenue from existing accounts and new business created by sales and supported by every other department in the organization. Everybody learns how to work together: Bert in sales, Roy in sales management, Bill in accounting, Carla in payroll, Ken in production, even HR. It's easy for everyone to pull together when inertia is overcome, and the thrill of the ride is new. Big smiles all around!

Your company successfully weathers normal adversities and becomes financially stable. In this stage, the more you sell, the more you're going to sell. You produce successful results for clients, and the reputation of you and your company spreads. This opens more doors and also makes them easier to close. You develop many happy client references to show your prospects.

Your income becomes predictable. You improve your standard of living. After several years of successful income growth, you feel financially secure enough to buy a newer car. You upgrade the furniture in your home, maybe even move to a different neighborhood. Your job and your life are wonderful!

Genesis and Monarchy phases occurred at almost exactly the same rate in all five of my top sales jobs. In each case, the Genesis era of the first year or two were exciting and fun growth and discovery periods. It's like they helped us set ourselves up to really make hay when the sun shone during Monarchy.

The Monarchy period made us all wealthy. We knew the business from the ground up because we pretty much grew with the company as it evolved. By then, we understood that we knew what it took to sell successfully, and we leveraged that knowledge and experience to sell more accounts and bigger accounts than ever before.

The Monarchy stage usually lasts one to two years beyond Genesis.

The Management Phase

Around the fifth year of a new business, you may pick up telltale signs of curious changes within your company. You wonder why messages from the top change in tone and tenor to become more formal, more distant, less personal, less enthusiastic, more pedantic, more official, and more "correct." You wonder why policies are instituted that seem limiting to successful *esprit de corps,* and why so many new responsibilities are heaped upon you and the sales team.

Your company expands staff to handle increased production created by more new clients and more new business revenue (i.e. sales). More people are needed in almost every department to handle the increased workload. The Suits install another new layer of management with the typical explanation that this is "due to the outstanding growth of our company."

The Boss morphs into an honest-to-God executive, the Captain at the helm of your ship. She isn't as available to participate at the ground level. She has bigger things on her plate. Her company has grown, and so has her job.

This is not at all a knock. It's exciting growth. During Genesis, you likely report directly to The Boss. During Monarchy, a sales manager is promoted from within for more direct support of the sales team at ground level. Sound business.

But a year or two later, you and your sales manager get knocked down an additional peg by the addition of a new Sales Suit, usually someone brought in from the outside who doesn't know your business like you do and who wasn't part of the growing pains from Day One. Odds are the new Suit feels compelled to justify his job.

This new Suit creates an additional stratum of bureaucracy between you and The Boss, which is new to you. If you want to have A Boss meeting, there are now two or more management levels above you so your former ability to walk in and talk directly to The Boss is considered inappropriate. Now you have to request a Skip Level Meeting.

Eventually, so many management positions are added that create so many new organizationally confining layers that your Suits run out of running room within their own departments. They start dropping in on other departments, like sales.

What makes a person think that because they manage one division of your company, they're qualified to stick their nose into your sales team, too?

Who's Who in the Zoo?

Your sales team begins getting called into meetings, not by your direct sales manager but by non-sales Suits who feel the need to throw their weight around. You wonder, *"Who's who in the zoo around here, anyway?"*

For example, you get an email from one of the Heap Big C-Suits along the lines of, "We have two more selling days in the month. We're behind. We have a lot of ground to make up. Make those calls! Send those emails! We can do this!"

Your first reaction is to respond as the loyal, positive professional that you are. You think, "You're right, Chief! Let's get this job done. We'll get the deals in! It'll be fun! It'll be exciting!"

Just one hour later, that very same C-Suit is on the phone with you, your entire sales team, and a host of others throughout your company. You yawn as your IT department head goes into great depth and detail about 21 new tech issues that could easily wait two days to be addressed. This conference call bores you until sleep drool pools on your desk so you find yourself doing what everyone else does: you press your mute button and surf the net.

The 90-minute discussion has almost zero relevance to your sales team, at least not on any timely basis compared to the C-Suit who's whipping the horses like it's the Kentucky Derby to "Make those calls! Send those emails!" the last couple days of the month.

Plus, you are unable to make the call to your prospect to close a deal because your only window of opportunity to catch him on the phone is shattered by this unwanted intrusion. And you don't just lose the active 90 minutes involved. There's prep time before and review time after that is unavailable for selling as well.

A full hour and a half of boring, irrelevant, techno-garble floats downstream, times 10 sales reps = 15 total selling hours—minimum—*Shinda*. Never to be seen again. And now you have fewer than two days left in the month to close deals.

Who calls that meeting? The IT department head who, though a really good guy and truly a genius at every aspect of his job, has no concept of sales, deals, deadlines, revenue goals, or the focus and concentration that occurs in sales the last few selling days of a month or quarter.

Here's a novel idea: maybe hold the dissemination of new general information about software, copier machine protocols, or the company's paper clip budget until the first day of the following month—two days away—*after* the critical sales deadlines for the month or the quarter or possibly the year have passed?

Boss, please: this policy change can be addressed and concluded in one short company-wide declaration.

Here's another scenario: The Marketing Suit announces a sudden conference call meeting with two days left in the sales QUARTER. During this 60-minute intrusion on your sales time, your team receives the exciting announcement that this morning the marketing department launched a slew of new and exciting online ads. That means the sales team will begin to receive calls and emails in response. Top priority is to be given to these new leads "effective immediately."

New inbound leads are prized commodities by any sales team, but this is another action that should be planned and executed a couple days later on the first day of the next month or the previous week. In any case, it should happen *before or after the last two selling days left in the QUARTER* when you and every Suit above you need to totally focus on closing deals you've been working on to this point.

A marketing department that creates initiatives producing valuable inbound leads is an extremely valuable part of any company. New sales leads are vital life's-blood to sales reps and need to be contacted as soon as possible when they come in. Every single minute helps, and every sales rep worth their salt knows this.

One of the highest priority tasks for a sales rep is to respond to every new lead quickly and professionally. But this *pales in comparison* to the importance of doing what needs to be done to get a deal closed, signed, brought in, recorded, and posted. Not to mention, paid. This isn't a new concept. Since about 1530, we've heard Hugh Rhodes' proverbial expression, "A bird in hand is worth ten flye at large." (Or, a bird in the hand is worth two in the bush.)

Last Word

If Your Boss lacks the experience to know that closed deals (results) are more important than new inbound leads (PROCESS), they need to find another job—or you do.

So What?

So there sits your sales team, like a bunch of frogs in a pot that's being very, very slowly brought to a boil. The frogs don't feel the temperature change because the heat increases so slowly and gradually. They just sit in the pot until they boil to death.

From the Management phase forward, the heat gradually gets turned up, and your company becomes increasingy structured by new Suits who justify their jobs with reports, meetings, spreadsheets, and anything else they can think up to document that they're actually doing something.

This evolution either triggers additional new layers of management, reports, and meetings, or it creates a sale opportunity for your company to sell to a different outfit for any number of different reasons. I can assure you that neither of these outcomes has anything to do with your professional welfare. If a new company buys yours, you can bet the new outfit will place its Prior Preferred Stock into positions currently held by your team.

How can you read the tea leaves to determine if it's time to adapt and overcome or leave? Please, proceed...

Mired Gun

In which we identify curious changes within your company, expose the corporate geek jargon of your Suits, examine how to know these changes are not in your interest, not for the better, and what you can do about your situation

Observe the Telltales

Dictionary.com defines "telltale" as:

> 1. A person who heedlessly or maliciously reveals private or confidential matters; tattler; talebearer.
> 2. *Yachting.* (on a sailboat) a feather, string, or similar device, often attached to the port and starboard shrouds and to the backstay, to indicate the relative direction of the wind. (HG Note: Literally used to read which way the winds are blowing).

In this chapter, we address both types of telltales, literal and metaphorical, as they relate to business settings.

Telltale #1: The Mole in Your Midst

A colleague in sales works at his desk late one Friday afternoon when one of the women in the office cheerfully swings by his Boof with a couple of beers in hand. The company graciously provides a generous monthly "snack" allowance that includes beer in the kitchen area refrigerator. These comforting morsels are all openly available to anyone in the office.

This woman places an unsolicited beer bottle on your colleague's desk and says in a jovial mood, "Happy Friday!" He thanks her for it and turns back to his tasks at hand. Only a few minutes later, his phone rings. It's one of your C-Suits calling him from the company's headquarters 1,500 miles away.

The C-Suit demands, "Stop whatever you're doing. I want you to go where you can call me on your cell phone, right now."

He parks his projects, walks out to his car, and dials the C-Suit from his mobile device. The C-Suit chastises his "drinking on the job" to the extent that your colleague worries about whether he's being fired. He says later this is such a strong verbal attack he knows it's useless to explain or try to defend himself. His only effective course of action is to sit tight and take the beating against the ropes until the bell rings.

Toward the end of the tongue-lashing, the Suit concludes with,

"And don't even try to find out who the Mole is!"

To your C-Suit's credit, all he knows is he's sitting in his office half a continent away from your office when he gets a smoke signal from the company's **Mole**. If I'm The Boss or even a reasonable facsimile thereof and learn that someone is "drinking on the job" at the office, I might be pissed off, too. To your C-Suit's further credit, moving your friend outside and away from the sales floor is an expert professional move, in keeping with this exec's typical refined and respectful acumen.

This isn't about the C-Suit receiving a notification and being put in the unfortunate, uncomfortable position of determining a course of action.

This is about—**the Mole.**

This situation occurred at a great company with many excellent programs to foster open communication between employees. The executive staff is a formidable collection of leaders and innovative minds, and this colleague is a Hired Gun—an excellent professional sales rep. The C-Suit is an unusual combination of formally educated corporate executive and outstanding salesperson. He consistently does the biggest deals in the company with high profile growth acquisitions.

Yet even in this positive environment, this incident involves an admitted **Company-Placed Mole** and occurs in an organization that proudly touts its verisimilitude of transparency. The company's progressive mindset toward employees is such that it provides a specific budget for beer onsite. It's also a company that installs **Moles** to tattle on others in the office when they have a beer.

I suggest you **most definitely find out who the Mole is in your operation.**

Otherwise, what's to prevent Your Suits from setting you up and framing you with a scenario like this one for someone to whack you?

The point is, find out if your company has installed a **Mole** in your office, department, sales team, etc. Then, as soon as possible and as subtly as possible, find out who that is. This is one hand that you'll want to play with your cards held closely to your vest.

Your next step is to determine a strategic course of action. To do otherwise is to choose to keep your head in the sand, as opposed to choosing to take control of your daily work environment for your own good.

It's up to you to decide what to do with your **Mole**. Basically, you have three choices:

1) Keep the *status quo*—you do nothing.

2) Acknowledge that you're on to them. Do you take them for a one-on-one ride just to get away from the typical office setting, of course, and politely counsel them on the possible consequences of a Mole's actions?

(Personally, I'd like to give them an up close and personal tour of *Mulholland Falls.*)

3) Or, do you completely mask the fact that you're wise to them?

Maybe instead, you decide to hang back and play their game so they blow their whistle about information you actually *want* them to pass along? *Spy versus Spy*.

Information is power.

— Law of the Hired Gun

The First Four Years

You probably know the rule of The First Four Seconds, the notion you only have one chance to make a good first impression. My extrapolation of this four second principle is that you often have about four years to truly assess your company and determine whether you remain to adapt and overcome, or leave. You only have one opportunity for The First Four Seconds; you only have one opportunity for the first four years, as well.

In the past era of American business, that might have sounded like sacrilege. You were supposed to enter a company in the mailroom, work your way up the ladder, and navigate internal politics the rest of your life to one day retire, and receive some token of respect and appreciation for your loyalty and dedication over all those years (the classic "gold watch" has become devalued to something like a *Thank You* thumb drive).

Based on that concept, I thought my average tenure of about 4½ years at my best sales positions looked a bit like a journeyman, but the average career lifespan at jobs across the board today is only 4.2 years and far shorter for millennials.

In the June 2016 Forbes article "Salespeople Are Burning Out Faster Than Ever -- Here's Why," writer Christine Comaford explains:

> According to Glassdoor, professionals working in sales can make well into the six figures and are one of the most popular positions companies seek to fill. But retention tends to be low with the pressure to meet numbers, lack of adequate training and inevitable rejection.

And there is a minimum 20 percent turnover in Sales—and it's up to 34 percent if you include both voluntary + involuntary according to Bridge Group research.

Millennials are even more likely to turnover:

25 percent say they'll leave their current job within a year; 44 percent say they'll leave within two years. (*The 2016 Deloitte Millennial Survey*)

51 percent will look for a new job at another organization in the next year. (*CEB/Clearside - Attracting & Retaining Millennials*)

In the *SAAS AE 2017 Metrics and Compensation Research Report*, The Bridge Group states, "Virtually unchanged since 2010, average rep tenure sits at 2.4 years."

Simply add the sum of your duration during the Genesis and Monarchy stages in your company, and plan your personal and professional strategy. Genesis: 1-3 years + Monarchy: 1-2 years = 2-5 years total maximum fun time in sales in one company. Somewhere in that range is how long you'll stay if you're fortunate enough to join a good outfit at the outset and remain productive during this brief dynasty of excellence.

Nevertheless, after about four years, you begin to pick up clues that don't make sense. But you don't delve too deeply into the circumstances behind these changes. Your focus is on your immediate matters at hand: Your job, sales, that next deal. That's why you're so successful.

It's also why you might get shot.

Telltale #2: Internal Memos and Corporate-Speak

During Genesis, internal memos usually are fun to get. They're from The Boss or your sales manager, and they present new ideas to help grow sales. Often, they're handwritten notes that congratulate you or the team for closing an important deal or setting a new sales record.

They carry sincere personal compliments and sometimes are replaced by a congratulatory phone call directly to you from The Boss. They go like this:

"Jack, great job landing the deal with Huge Elephant Consolidated. Glad you're on our team!" ~ *The Boss*

But after Genesis and Monarchy, the tone and timbre of the messages change. It takes you awhile to pick up on the differences, but one change is that the memos are no longer handwritten notes, they no longer come to you directly from The Boss, and they aren't notes personally directed to just you. Instead, they come to your whole sales team from one of many Suits or Junior Wannabe Suits. They morph from active tense to passive tense, and rarely cite individual names. They employ correct robotic HR geek-speak, like these:

"Management has decided..."

"The decision has been made..."

"Management hasn't gotten back to me yet..."

"That's currently under discussion..."

Mostly, these internal memos only deal with numbers and/or geek-speak terms employed to effectively obfuscate the real issues at hand. You feel like you need a translator to decipher them.

The Wit and Wisdom of Fred G. Sanford

In the immortal TV sitcom, *Sanford and Son,* two local uniformed police officers called "Smitty" and "Swanny" drop by from time to time to help Fred Sanford and his son, Lamont, at their junk shop. Swanny is a pedantic by-the-book cop who uses the officially approved police vernacular to describe everything to the nth degree. Swanny's partner, Smitty, is streetwise and translates Swanny's cop-speak for Fred Sanford.

For example, in one scene Fred believes he has whiplash after being rear-ended.

Fred:

Ain't it true I can sue when I get this whiplash, Swanny?

Swanny:

Speaking off the record, I can only tell you that in the case where Vehicle One is struck from behind by Vehicle Two the occupant of Vehicle One is in the legal optimal position to obtain monetary compensation from the occupant of Vehicle Two, that party being liable for all damages incurred by the occupant of Vehicle One.

Fred looks helplessly at Smitty for an interpretation.

Smitty:
Brother, you're sittin' on top of a gold mine!

Or this:

A burglar breaks into Fred's house while he's asleep at night. When Fred's son Lamont comes home, he wakes Fred and startles the crook. The burglar flees and drops his gun to the floor as he vamooses.

Fred and Lamont try to sell the gun at a pawn shop, but the pawnbroker thinks Fred is holding him up with the gun and signals the police. Officers Smitty and Swanny arrive on the scene and question the pawnbroker.

Lamont:
Hey wait a minute, Smitty. I don't know what he's talking about. All we did was come in here to pawn this gun that we found.

Swanny:
You found that gun?

Lamont:
Yeah, last night. We surprised a burglar when we came home early. He dropped it as he ran out.

Swanny:
I think I should advise you that the failure to report a breaking and entering and to relinquish a firearm to the authorities constitutes a felonious act. However, since you have no criminal record, we'll nullify the usual accusatory procedures.

Fred and Lamont look at Smitty.

Smitty:
We're not gonna bust you.

I feel similar to Fred Sanford when I get internal memos from Above that foretell the end of the Monarchy phase and the beginning of a company's Management phase. Below are some examples of what I mean, as seen in actual Management phase memos. I've quoted them verbatim on the left and added my "Smitty-esque" interpretations on the right.

We can model this for your agency with some inputs so you have expected ROI leveraging the online sourcing technology.	*You can show Your Boss how you're making money.*
Analyzing some customer data our technology delivers programs for one dollar per unit taken.	*It costs a buck a book.*
The administrator will coach a department as a Balance Agent using evidence-based processes to implement XXX/YYY/ZZZ programs to restore social equilibrium using assessment matrix and quantitative metrics.	*I'm making this up as I go along.*

My first question is, "Do you guys stay up late at night just to come up with this stuff?"

I'm sure the cocktail hour Suits are impressed by these intra-office missives as they sniff their wines and impress each other with corporate geek jargon about the trendy new "best practices" they put into place at their companies. I can assure you there is a far greater number of people who roll their eyes, like the members of the sales team who have to decipher this contrived corporate geek jargon, just like Fred G. Sanford. There is one common denominator though: Fred deals in junk and so do the Suits. Geek-Junk.

Telltale #3: Memos from Helicopter Managers

Here's a short list of quotes from actual internal memos. When you see these creep into the daily lexicon of company communications, it should help you identify whether there are healthy winds in your company's sails or turbulent weather ahead:

- Effective immediately
- You are required to follow business and manager directives
- Follow protocol
- You are required to get manager approval
- Turn in reports in a timely fashion
- Send me a report by EOB each Friday with the same information above
- List of Dos & Don'ts:
  (HG note: Brought to you by the Do-Be and Don't-Be Romper Room School of Business Management)
- Sales territories are being restructured (i.e. reduced)
- New sales targets will be announced (i.e. your quota is going up)
- Multi-year deals are no longer accepted. (*Hidden Message: You just lost 33 percent of your income*)
- Commissions on account renewals have been discontinued. (*Overt Message: You just lost 2 percent of your income*)
- Do not ask or bargain with colleagues

Telltale #4: Your CRM Becomes Your Company's G.O.D.

At one company, we changed our contact management system to The Greatest CRM* in the World. We knew that was a valid claim because that's what the CEO, COO, Suits, and managers all told us. Everybody loved it, except the salespeople who were forced to actually endure its multitudinous pedantic boxes to fill out on each and every call, all day, every day. But it produced great reports!

*(CRM = Customer Resource Management solution, hereinafter referred to in this book as: *G.O.D.* Microsoft (dynamics.microsoft.com) explains CRM this way: "A strong CRM solution is a multifaceted platform where everything crucial to developing, improving, and retaining your customer relationships is stored."

As we grew, it became increasingly important to the Suits for us to complete all the steps in our heavenly CRM to document the electronic trail of events that led up to the completion of each sale, like dropping crumbs along the path to find our way home. That way, they could pull progress reports that showed how many deals were on their way to getting done.

It wasn't right anymore just to sell a deal. You had to provide electronic fingerprints along each step of the CRM's electronic paper trail. CRM became *G.O.D.*—all-knowing, all-seeing, all-reporting, all-encumbering. All of this was necessary to justify management's expensive purchase of a CRM that shackled the ankles of the entire sales team, daily.

Was there any input toward the final decision to buy this CRM from the salespeople who had to live with it and operate within its restrictive structure? Who researched the CRM? Who discussed the options? Who made the buying decision? Your Suits. Why did they choose that one? Because it does a great job of providing them with myriad and manifold REPORTS. Not because it streamlines the functionality of the sales PROCESS.

Frankly, I can outproduce most of the current overpriced CRMs on sales call volume and quality conversations per day with a box of 5 x 7 index cards with tab dividers numbered for each day of the month and each month of the year. But this doesn't provide good reports. It just gets the job done. It sells.

> HIRED GUN GUARANTEE: Mention this old-school alternative system to your Suits and watch their heads explode. After you pitch your idea, just sit back and say, "Mm-hmm" each time they protest. You may hear something like this:
>
> 1) What they think *you* want to hear: "That'll never work for you."
> "Mm-hmm."

2) What they think *they* want to hear: "It's way too limited in its depth of information." "Mm-hmm."

3) The *truth*: "But we can't produce reports with that!"

The end result of implementing *G.O.D.*? Across the board, outbound sales call volume fell because it took so long to move from one sales call to the next due to the inordinate granular details required to be reported on each call. We also received email missives with pedantic Kiddy Talk that instructed us in minute detail about how strongly we were required to fall in line with this mind-numbing PROCESS.

Here are some email examples, with the names of the identifiable sales phases in *G.O.D.* put in terms that align with this kindergarten level of PROCESS management.

When you document call activity in *G.O.D.*, use the *Cans & String* box to indicate a call where you had a two-way conversation. Voice mail messages or live messages do not count as two-way conversations. The *Romper Room* box should be used if you leave a voicemail. Continue to use the box for *Show & Tell* when you have a demo, and the *Pow Wow* box if you meet in person. Reply directly to acknowledge receipt of this message.

This is a good reason why all stages need to be marked in *G.O.D.* with all activities. This account is still marked in the *Preschool* stage and it is very unlikely a sale ever closes on a *Preschool* call. *(HG note: I personally closed 25 out of 70 deals the previous year in that same* Preschool *stage...)*

This account shows still in *Preschool* status, very unlikely a sale would close in a *Preschool* call.... They must have a *Building Block* stage, then *Cans & String*, then *Show & Tell* to be close to being a true opportunity to close soon.

Some of these dogmatic directives come to you from your Junior Suit telling you that you cannot possibly close a deal unless you follow a specific step-by-step PROCESS. You can't just call or email, then sign someone up—you must *first* make them jump through a hula hoop, then a basketball hoop, then a hoop covered in ice, then a flaming hoop (in that order), and each hoop stage *must* be fully and completely documented in *G.O.D.* Otherwise, it just cannot possibly be a done deal.

Why? So your Junior Suits can produce myriad REPORTS in *G.O.D.* that show how many deals are allegedly in each hoop stage when they defend their jobs in Suit meetings.

When I sold high-tech software that revolutionized the direct mail service bureau industry, one of my sales colleagues there helped a lot teaching me the technology, business, and sales strategy. He was one of the most vivacious people I've known. He always made me laugh, and he closed more deals than I did. He was, without doubt, one of the best in-the-field, high-tech reps I've known. When he retired, we had a long phone call about our sales time together, and he emailed me the following note:

> Early CRM solutions wanted to prove to management that X number of phone calls, direct mails, trade shows, mailers, con-calls, presentations, and quotes will deliver a sale every time.
>
> Sales managers were driven to activity, not results. Once management gets hooked on their CRM then you see the circle of lies begin. Sales reps lie to cover their asses on worthless activities.
>
> Sales managers present a rosy future based on # of activities.... Senior managers report to shareholders the bright and shining future...just look at all these (mindless) activities.
>
> What is flawed is that the information loaded into the CRM was based on good, solid sales activities. Yes, 30 proposals got 25 orders because the sales PROCESS and steps were solid. Now, you throw out those successful activities and replace them with mindless drills; the numbers start to lie.
>
> Example: "Look, VP Bob, last year we sold $5 million with 200 written proposals, with our new

> CRM we are SHOWING that we have X phone calls, X leads, X direct mails...based on this new info, we are about to have the best year ever! **Idiots. The only winner was the guy that sold them the CRM!"**

An experienced, successful sales manager knows this and works to improve the skills of the incompetent rep while finding ways to help the successful rep spend more time doing what's important—selling—instead of filling out a bunch of boxes on spreadsheets to justify the Sales Suit's job.

Telltale #5: The Reports

During Genesis and for most of Monarchy, there are few reports, if any. The only thing you bother with, or that anyone bothers with, is that everybody does as much as they can all day every day. It's all hands on deck at all times.

It's one of the most fun and exciting times of your life. It's exciting because during Genesis and most of Monarchy, all there is to do is sell! There are no time-sapping impediments to sales like reports, reports, and more reports. Everyone in the company does as much as they can to bring in revenue as fast as it can be acquired.

In these first years, revenue goals get obliterated monthly. This means high fives and celebratory drinks at the local watering hole after the last day of each month. The only sales report necessary to see is The Big Board O' Deals.

But later, in a post-Monarchy company with one or more new levels of management in place, things change. New **Sales Reports** creep into your life. They quickly grow in number in direct proportion to the expansion of your company and the number of Suits who have to justify their jobs by showing a lot of spreadsheets and data in meetings.

Before you realize it, so many reports are heaped upon you so often and from so many different directions that you hardly have time to make calls and sales. The time and energy required to complete all the new reports take that time and energy away from your core task of selling.

In their *2015 SaaS Inside Sales Survey Report,* The Bridge Group reports, "On average, reps are having 6.6 conversations per day. This is down from 9.5 in 2012—that's nearly a 34 percent drop.... [We] have found that more conversations per day is correlated with higher quota attainment. (*And yes, we did find statistical significance p= .05.*)"

The Bridge Report adds: "We aren't willing to offer a cause for this drop. But we will caution—**this matters**."

According to a research report by Clearside and CSO Insights, "*7 Sales Leader Insights to Improve Performance in 2016*," the amount of time a salesperson spends actually selling is 35 percent.

Why are the number of dials, conversations, and sales dropping?

I don't think it takes a theoretical physicist to figure it out, so let your friendly neighborhood Hired Gun venture a wild guess. When you're spending all your time doing sales forecasts, pipeline reports, expense reports, activity reports, CRM reports, and sitting in on meetings and conference calls, the time available to make sales calls drops so sales drop.

When sales drop, each new, insecure Suit in every new layer of management scrambles to justify their job. They add even more sales impediments in efforts to document to the higher-ups that there really are *all these deals out there*! The irony is they think this shows The Boss how well they're managing their reps. What it shows me is that management has no clue how to lead salespeople.

The more you lead, the less you manage. The more you manage, the less you lead.

— Law of the Hired Gun

When this transformation within your company begins, you typically receive emails from the Suit who creates the new reports with detailed instructions on how to complete each one. These are copied to everyone on God's Green Earth, most especially The Boss and all other C-Suits.

Telltale #6: Emails and Universal Replies to Everyone!

These sales/forecast/pipeline reports are generally followed by the emergence of **Activity Reports**. Because sales drop under the weight of so many Suit-created sales impediments, these additional distracting reports are created to document how much work you're actually doing.

That way, they have evidence you're showing up to work, making calls, sending emails, and filling out reports. The bogus management theory is that these reports will indicate the quantity of activities that should lead to sales or the lack thereof.

In their carefully orchestrated spreadsheet boxes, your new activity reports show how many calls you make, how many pitches you make, how many demos you give, how many meetings you have, and so forth. Everything except the number of deals you close and the revenue you generate for the company.

It isn't enough that you're already busting your butt to make as many sales as possible. You're already making as many calls to new prospects, delivering as many demos, sending as many emails, and participating in as many client meetings as you can.

Now more of your precious time is leached away to deal with another new report. This one is intended to document how much work you're doing, despite all the distractions caused by endless reports.

I've never understood the relevancy of **Activity Reports**. If you show you only made two sales calls, yet you delivered $2 million in new revenue, what does that activity report prove? If you show you made 200 sales calls, and you have a big goose egg on the board, do you think the documentation of 200 sales calls means anything? (Yes, it means you can't sell!) I've got news for them:

Activity does not guarantee results.

— Law of the Hired Gun

Making a high number of calls, sending a high number of emails, and delivering a high number of demos does not ensure successful results.

Let me repeat that: Making a high number of calls, sending a high number of emails, and delivering a high number of demos does not ensure successful results.

If the salesperson is a crummy rep, higher numbers only indicate more prospects burned by that crummy rep.

Conversely, an excellent rep may make half the number of calls or send half the number of emails as the incompetent rep yet deliver twice the sales.

Telltale #7: Expense Reports

"A Few Good Expenses" is a funny sales video with Chris Pappas and Anthony Emmanouil that parodies *A Few Good Men.* It's set in the final courtroom scene where Tom Cruise cross examines Jack Nicholson as the Marine Colonel in charge of Guantanamo Bay.

Colonel:
You want answers?

Cruise:
I think I'm entitled.

Colonel:
You want answers?

Cruise:
I want the truth!

Colonel:
You can't handle the truth. Son, we live in a world that requires revenue. And that revenue must be brought in by people with elite skills. Who's going to find it? You, Mr. Finance? You, Mr. Operations? We have a greater responsibility than you could possibly fathom.

You scoff at the sales division. You curse our lucrative incentives. You have that luxury. You have the luxury of not knowing what we know: That while the costs of business results may seem excessive, it drives in revenue. And my very existence, while grotesque and incomprehensible to you, drives revenue.

You don't want to know the truth because deep down in places that you don't talk about in team and management meetings, you want me on that call. You need me on that call.

We use words like Freeview and volume control, total cost of ownership. We use these words as the backbone of a life spent negotiating something. You use them as a punchline.

I have neither the time nor inclination to explain myself to people who rise and sleep under the very blanket of revenue that I provide, and then question the manner in which I provide it. I would rather you just said, "Thank You," and went on your way.

Otherwise, may I suggest you pick up the phone and make some sales calls! Either way, I don't give a damn what you think you're entitled to.

Cruise:
Did you expense the lap dances?

Colonel:
I did the job I was hired to do.

Cruise:
Did you expense the lap dances?!

Colonel:
You're (G.D.) right I did!

To quote that celebrated genius of business and commerce, Forest Gump: "And that's all I have to say about that."

Telltale #8: Meetings

Your meetings during Genesis are once a week with your sales manager, and they last about 15 minutes. They're results oriented;

they deal with adversities encountered by sales reps in the field, and they focus on tactics and doing deals.

Now, in your post-Monarchy "Mature Market" company, meetings are called much more frequently, often without notice. Within the first three hours of your workday, you receive **FIVE** emails from your C-Suit about meetings. You also receive **THREE** emails from your Sales Suit about meetings. Just to make sure, you also have a quick **phone call** from your friendly neighborhood Sales Suit to make sure you read the **THREE** emails about the meetings. Which meetings?

Bi-weekly one-on-one meetings
Monthly team meetings
Ad hoc sales roundtable meetings
Tech update meetings
New team member intro meetings
State of the company meetings
Quarterly kickoff meetings
TED talk viewing and discussion meetings
Optional to attend meetings (Followed by an impromptu one-on-one with a Suit about why you opted not to attend.)

Telltale #9: Check-in Calls

It isn't enough that you have in-person sales meetings to discuss all your accounts and their status in-depth, plus weekly account status reports on spreadsheets, but then come the "check-in calls." The point of these calls: What have you done for me lately? And what will you do for me tomorrow? The exact same thing you went over in your meetings and spreadsheets, and exactly the same things you went over during the check-in call yesterday, and the day before that, and two days before that.

When these telephone drop-ins from your manager begin, they occur about once a week. Then, as the Management phase grows, its multiple tentacles grip all the departments in your organization. It slowly squeezes from the top down, and pressure increases throughout the company, pushing some people out the back door.

That's when Suits play CYA (Cover Your Ass): "If I make the sales team show on a bunch of reports that they either are or aren't performing activities and that they are or aren't projecting sales, it's them! Not me! If they don't deliver, it isn't *my* fault!"

The reports grow more detailed and didactic, and the volume of check-in calls increases. On top of that, you also start receiving these same check-in calls from *other* company Suits in other *non-sales* departments.

Telltale #10: Sales Forecasts

Every week, you're asked, "Your target revenue for this month is XYZ. What do you have in your current pipeline that will get you there?"

How do people respond? They make stuff up!

You have a number of deals working, and those at the top of your pipeline report spreadsheets are the most likely to come in. Because these reports are reviewed openly in meetings with your peers, you want them to be good.

In your sales meeting, your Sales Suit goes around the conference table, and each rep cites their prospective deals and the anticipated revenue along with their odds of coming in this month as a done deal.

What good does this do? How does this help you sell more? How does this help any other sales reps sell more? Aren't those supposed to be the reasons for "sales meetings"? Remember this time-honored *Law of the Hired Gun*:

Meetings are called for the benefit of the person who calls the meeting.

— Law of the Hired Gun

This isn't a sales meeting. It's a Suit meeting called to justify the job of the Suit, not for the benefit of the sales team members. They check their email accounts and upcoming calls in *G.O.D.* while each rep bores everyone except the Suit with their tales of sales that *should be coming in.*

This creates an environment where more prospects are added to the lists to pad the projections. When this happens, and one of them drops off the list, you pray to Saint Expedite to save your butt, possibly with a bluebird deal that flies in just in the nick of time.

The last thing you want to do is let them know about any particularly sizable deal you're working on that looks like it will come in. If you do let the Suits in on it, you know that about five times a day you're going to have to answer the question, "How is your big deal looking?" or "Is that big deal of yours coming in today?" or "Have you heard from your big deal today?" The Suits pester the living hell out of you if they know you have a good-sized deal imminent because they want to find a way for it to make them look good.

Who makes up these target numbers anyway? Where do they come from? Just what is the magic formula used by the Suits in your company to determine precisely how much you should be generating in new and total revenue for the planned current operation and future growth of the organization? How much input does sales have regarding the new numbers its team members are expected to hit?

I could have sworn I heard someone say,

"We're a Transparent Company"

Tell it to the tourists. This is voluntarily offered up so it's on the record that you heard them say it but you don't see much convincing evidence that it's actually true. It's the same as Nixon saying, "I'm not a crook."

How many times has someone told you, "I'm an honest guy," before they try to pull a fast one on you? Maybe you've heard, "It's been a long time since I've played cards," as they three-finger the deck and deal off the bottom or someone says, "I'm just a small-town country lawyer," as they try to get you to sign documents that part you from your money. Or, my favorite, "I'm really not making any money on this deal." And then there's also, "Now this will only hurt a little bit."

Every time I hear someone tell me that they are transparent, it isn't long before they become expert in complicating the few truly important things I want to know. Oh sure, they offer up all kinds of minutia about irrelevant, unimportant things in the manner that a modern submarine jettisons multiple defensive decoys against incoming threats. Or they lie by omission and offer up inconsequential information but don't directly address the question at hand.

But ask about something truly important, like *why* your commission structure has to change in the first place, or exactly *what formula* is used to determine your revised sales commission plan, or your annual projected increase in your targeted sales revenue, and you hear: *Oh my, oh my, oh my!* You're being blasphemous, sacrilegious, and not a team player!

Do the top Suits in your company like to beat their chests about their transparency? Fine, then share that revenue stream formula with us.

Is this new set of target numbers for sales devised by using an actuarial formula determined by your crack team of CEO, COO, CFO, EVP, Sales Manager, and sales team members based on the projected stock dividend amount required to be earned by the company's "ask" stock price to shareholders deduced through analysis of current and anticipated future industry trends and your company's total operating budget?

NAWP! Most probably not, but if it is, I'd like to see it.

Do they also like to boast about their aspirations to hit big new revenue goals each year? Great! Say, just how are those goals derived and set? Based on what, exactly? I'm just asking for some transparency here because I'm one of the people you're going to approach when you want to know how much revenue is coming in to hit *YOUR* goal.

Did members of the sales team have any real, meaningful input as to what target numbers they're assigned to achieve next year? Or were the new, carefully computed numbers merely shown to the sales reps so they could acquiesce and sign off on them?

Where is the transparency that shows exactly how and why these new numbers are determined?

And if the company is making such huge revenue increases and boasting about it year after year, why aren't I making more money than I did the year before, or the year before that?

If you dare to ask any of these questions, you won't get the answers you seek. Instead, you will witness a smooth little sidestep to a diversion tactic like, "Why are you asking these questions? Is there something you doubt about the company? What are your concerns?"

Deny. Deflect. Defend. Classic.

The next thing you'll hear them say might sound something like, "You don't need an attorney—that's what you have us for!"

It's Always Good to Have a Friend Who's an Attorney

I was 22 when we bought our first home. I didn't know much about real estate deals. All I knew was that we signed a contingency contract with a 60-day out to purchase a nice home, which meant that we couldn't close on the deal or move in until the people living there actually sold it.

One afternoon, I got a phone call from the two real estate agents who handled our deal. They asked me to come by their office. They wanted to run something by me and have me sign some new documents. After reading through the papers, I couldn't quite put my finger on what was going on, but I knew I already had a signed deal in hand and felt uncomfortable about the whole thing.

"I have a friend in law school here focusing on contract law," I said. "I'd like to have him take a look at these before I sign anything."

The two agents actually looked at me and replied, "You don't need an attorney—that's what you have us for!"

An hour later, they tried to schmooze my Phi Beta Kappa track team buddy with a lot of Happy Talk as he read the documents. He stopped and announced, "There is absolutely no way I would have him sign this. This is an open-ended contract with no time limits that binds him to the purchase of that house if it takes 100 years!"

They were both fired by the broker, who put us up rent free in a nice apartment until the deal got done a month or so later.

Want to See Suits Do the Sidestep? Ask Questions

You hear Your Boss tout the transparency of your company. How transparent is that, actually?

Hired Gun: Can you tell me why our commission structure has to be changed in the first place?

Suit: Uh, no.

Hired Gun: It looks like we don't make as much money as we've been making.

Suit: Oh, but you do! If you hit 120 percent of your new (increased) quota number, you make more!

Hired Gun: Has anyone in the history of the company ever hit 120 percent of that number?

Suit: Uh, no.

Hired Gun: Can I look at the company's financial statement?

Suit: Uh, no.

Hired Gun: You keep telling us your goal for the company is to produce X million dollars by next year. How do you arrive at that number? What is it actually based on?

Suit: That's something we can talk about in a sideboard discussion.

Hired Gun: If we do produce X million dollars by next year, what does that mean to us? What does it mean to me?

Suit: That's also something we can talk about in a sideboard discussion.

Hired Gun: My job performance is measured and evaluated by the new sales revenue numbers you guys project. As a professional salesperson, that seriously affects and concerns me. I'd like to know how those projected sales increases are determined.

Suit: Why are you asking all these questions? Don't you trust us?

Hired Gun: Why won't you just answer the questions?

High achievers are similar to good actors who need to understand their characters' motivations. They need to understand what is behind a concept or challenge issued to them; they are not just clock-punching drones who take orders and don't think for themselves.

How High-Level Decisions Are Made

I don't remember a lot of details about my first meeting with one of The Bosses of the world's largest chain of convenience stores. I don't remember the size or decor of his office, the floor level, the name of his advertising manager, or the names of his outer office personnel. But this is what I do remember.

I bit the inside of one cheek. Then, when that got numb from pain, I bit the inside of the other cheek as I compressed my lips and averted my eyes. This Boss wasn't looking at me but out his window as he pondered rolling the dice on a brand new ad medium his company had not yet tried. The price tag of this initial trial run was more than the 2018 equivalent of $250,000.

Just one rung below T.H.E. Boss, he was a decision maker for many thousands of stores across the central US. This particular project covered their 1,300 locations throughout the Dallas-Fort Worth metroplex. He asked, "About how many homes would we target per store, on average?"

Their stores throughout DFW's fourth-ranked Metropolitan Statistical Area saturated the entire market, and there were several reasons why they would be best served by covering all of the 1.3 million available households. I waited for him to answer his own question. An hour-long minute later, he guessed, "About a thousand?"

I replied, "That's perfect. One thousand homes per store times 1,300 stores saturates the full DFW market of 1,300,000 homes. With a full market buy, we can assign your eight-page tab to the outside position of the entire bundle that we mail that week. For convenience, postal carriers often insert the smaller pieces of mail inside larger ones and roll them all together so the whole bundle rolls up and slides easily into the mailbox. Your tab will be on the outside of all the mail in 1.3 million DFW mailboxes that day. It will be the first thing seen in more than a million households when they get their mail."

"Let's do that."

Done deal.

Result: All stores completely sold out of many advertised items. My client Boss was a hero within the corporation, and news spread through their HQ hallways by word of mouth. Soon all Boss level execs had me in meetings with their ad teams. A company that never used print media advertising became one of our company's biggest clients nationwide and mailed over 50 million pieces with us each year. Every campaign averaged 1,000 households per store.

Believe me, your compensation plan is made with the same extensive intellectual thought, economic theory, and forensic analysis but quite possibly not by someone as shrewd as my convenience store client.

Telltale #11: New! Improved! Contracts for Clients to Sign

During Genesis, your clients sign a one-page document when they do a deal. The top half of the page is contact information for both companies entering into agreement. The bottom half contains terms and services described in one succinct paragraph. If you can get a deal done on a bar napkin, it flies.

When the Management phase curls its tentacles around the ankles of the sales team, a new impediment is born. The sales team is presented with new, legally updated versions of your standard contracts for clients to sign. These gems contain mandatory, highly visible links so prospects can read new legalese and "terms and conditions" more than 10 pages long. Ten pages of legal decrees and terms and conditions are imbedded into what was previously a one-page document that stated everything clearly in plain English and was easy to get signed by your decision maker.

You know the Golden Era has passed and that Genesis and Mon archy are history when you work days, weeks, and months busting your ass to get a deal sold and in position to close only to get a call from your primary contact who needs to send this extensive paperwork to their black hole o' death legal department. It may take from six weeks to six months to come out again. If you're lucky.

You check in with your direct contact for status updates as creatively and as often as possible without antagonizing the one person who is the internal champion of moving the deal along. *Six months* go by. On your last cursory call to check on the deal's progress "with legal," you learn that your contact no longer works there. The deal never comes in. ***Shinda.***

Telltale #12: Contract Scrutiny

During Genesis and Monarchy, the deal flies even if you get it done on a cocktail napkin that you discover in your pocket while you're sobering up the next morning. Hell, it's probably framed and displayed in the sales room. In those halcyon days, when a deal comes in, it's celebrated.

But *now* you almost hate to turn in a new deal because you know you'll just get called in by a sales or accounting Suit and raked over hot coals while they review every single word and every punctuation point to make sure it fits in a box that is 100 percent *bona fide* according to *G.O.D.'s* "PROCESS."

You want to scream. You want to tell your Junior Suit to get his head out of his ass. You want to say, "You're right. Let's just tear up the signed contract and throw it out. We don't need that deal. I'll just go get a different one." When you finish tearing your hair out, you want to call The Boss and say, "Boss, we've worked together here for years since you hired me yourself. Just what the hell is going on?"

"Why is all this happening?"

Just one quick question: Has your company recently been acquired—or taken on new financing—such as new investors, a new partnership or vulture capital backers, or a second round of vulture capitalization? Or a third round?

Telltale #13: The New Investors

When new money is infused into your company, you can accurately anticipate that you will experience just about everything outlined above. New investments beget new modes of documentation within your company to justify and defend that investment back to the investors.

To you, that means meetings to pressure more sales, reports to pressure more sales, forecasts to pressure more sales, pipeline reviews to pressure more sales, check-in calls to pressure more sales, and role-playing sessions among five- and 10-year veteran sales reps to pressure more sales. Anything to pressure more sales. "We need more money—and we have to document how we're working hard to get it!"

Results are not the key anymore; PROCESS is all important. Sure, you need to hit numbers but during all your meetings and myriad distractions, how much time and effort is spent actually discussing Deals and Results versus discussing PROCESS?

Make your own decision but this is where I saddle up. I'm there to produce results. I'm not there to dance at the end of some marionette's strings, polishing reports to help Suits justify their jobs.

I was Regional Sales Manager in Dallas for a California company. Our sales territory was eight southwest and mountain states. A couple years after I started, we received news that our company was approved for a third round of venture capital financing. Upper management tried to spin it as a great thing. My question was, why is it a great thing to go back three times for funding?

Expansion is great. Growth is the goal of just about any company to become, as they say, "the dominant player in our vertical space." (Translation: We want to be the Big Dog in our industry.) Infusion of capital investment in order to grow and expand is standard business practice with a fair return going to the outfit that ponies up the ducats to fund that growth. But give me a break.

Over-aggressive expansion killed every one of the outstanding companies where I previously enjoyed great success, and where are they today? ***Shinda.***

Company Priorities:
#1 top external company priority:
New Business Revenue
#1 top internal company priority: Payroll

— Law of the Hired Gun

If you find that your organization does not hold these *Laws of the Hired Gun* priorities sacred, immediately find another job. Don't hope; don't wait. Get the hell out.

If the C-level execs value their spreadsheets more than incoming new revenue to pay the bills, you're cooked.

If those same C-level execs don't believe that payroll is #1, immediately find another job. They find out very quickly how important it is when they miss one paycheck to your company's employees.

Your company's revenue stream is built on the bones of bygone sales reps who came before you.

— Law of the Hired Gun

Letter of Resignation

Below is an actual letter of resignation that a disenfranchised sales rep in one of my top five sales jobs delivered to his direct report supervisor and every one of the Suits in upper management, including The Boss. It found its way to me after the author shared it with a number of us in the company. (BTW: This was written about six years after this fast-track company launched.)

"It has become increasingly apparent over the past 90 days that The Company's direction and structure are inconsistent with my personal goals for career growth," the letter reads. "Accordingly, please accept my resignation from The Company, effective immediately."

It goes on, "Several promotion opportunities have arisen since my joining The Company. With the much-heralded restructuring of the management team, several people have been promoted to positions in sales and marketing in our sales vertical. I expressed interest in each of these positions yet was never offered an interview. Having held vice president titles several times in my career with responsibility for annual sales of over $100 million, I was confident and assured a position would become available in the near future and felt my qualifications certainly merited even the most cursory review. However, in each case, I was either considered and subsequently rejected, or more likely, not even considered. In any event, The Company's propensity to hire from outside and my promotion potential have been clearly established.

"It has also become clear that our sales vertical enjoys a diminishing viability vis-a-vis its competitors, all of which have rolled out or will soon introduce products technologically superior to ours. In two (2) separate, detailed studies, I presented management a thorough summary analysis outlining our strengths and weaknesses. To date, no action has been taken, and management's response is to simply sell more. In a few words, our sales vertical has fallen seriously behind its competitors and lacks the desire to rectify, improve, or enhance its competitive positioning strategy. This conclusion was clearly evidenced by management's failure to support the presentation effort for a 14-site superstore chain.

"Further, it is now evident The Company has adopted or now tolerates a verification policy initiated by the accounting department, which is at extreme cross-purposes with sales. While accounting verification of contract terms and conditions with new customers may appear on the surface to serve the purpose of eliminating fraudulent contracts, it also provides the customer an implicit right to rescind and has negated the sale in virtually every instance. This policy appears to be firmly institutionalized in the accounting manner of thinking and has not varied despite numerous efforts to discuss the issue. An apologetic sales management team has been unwilling, or more specifically, unable to take action resulting in demonstrative change in this practice.

"Coincidentally, the random verifications are arbitrarily performed when a significant bonus threshold is reached. It is a well-known axiom that given an opportunity to change their minds, thirty to forty percent (30-40 percent) of all our customers will [do that] rather than accept the consequences of their purchase decision. The most recent manifestation of this ill-conceived policy has cost me over $5,000, my teammates $1,000, and The Company $15,000, a situation I find most untenable. The trend appears to be ever-increasing empowerment of accounting administration and disenfranchising of sales, to the detriment of Company growth. Not only is this trend disturbing and not deserving of management support, but its persistence sends an alarming signal that management remains unable to take actions that positively affect desired sales results without misdirected oversight from accounting skewing those results."

Ask yourself this question: How much time do your Suits actually invest in helping you sell deals versus the time they waste reviewing your sales PROCESS? Believe me, it's going to get worse before it gets better, if it ever does.

Sales is a dynamic, not a process.

— **Law of the Hired Gun**

About two to five years into your sales tenure with a company, you will pick up indications that things around you are changing and that some of those changes don't make sense. Remember one of the primary *Laws of the Hired Gun*: whenever anything doesn't make sense, follow the money.

So What?

Do not just observe, mutter that these changes seem to get curiouser and curiouser, shrug your shoulders, and go back to work, even if that seems a model of focus and commitment to excellence.

It's not. It's closing your eyes while the blindfold gets slipped over your head, and you're about to get shot. For your own good and for control over your own life, take a step back, and allow a few moments for the smoke to clear to provide a clear vision of what's taking place around you.

Measure your values and beliefs against these telltale signs, and contemplate your future direction. Hell, even a condemned man gets to pause and enjoy a last cigarette. Take a moment to have your cigarette equivalent, and reflect, analyze, and plan.

It may be the best time for new people to join this outfit.

It may be the best time for you to stay.

It also may be past the time you should saddle up and ride out of town.

Observe what's going on around you; figure out the reasons why. Then do something about it: Join a different division, remain where you are, adapt and overcome, or leave. Make it your decision. Take control of your career and your life.

Levity Break

Top ten things you will never hear a Hired Gun sales rep say:

10 We need to slow down the overperformers so the underperformers can catch up.
9 We need more Suits around here.
8 Please increase my quotas.
7 Please give me a new spreadsheet form to do.
6 I'd like accounting to call my new deals to ask if they want to cancel.
5 I need to reduce my sales territory.
4 I don't have enough reports to do.
3 Can we please have another meeting today?
2 Can we add role-playing sessions to our meetings?
1 Can I please have a one-on-one with HR?

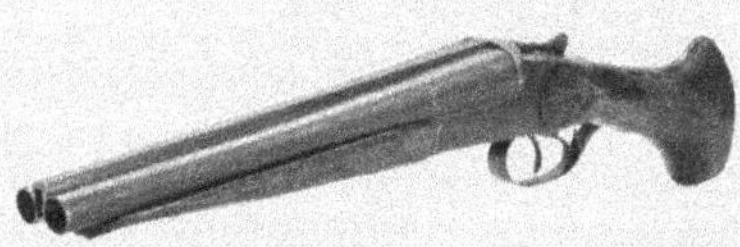

Fired Gun

In which we accept the fact that getting fired for making too much money is an occupational hazard in sales

"The upper management team had informed me that an employee [who] worked for me was a poor performer and would be terminated soon.... When I followed the company procedures and reported this to human resources, their response was to inform me that my contract would not be renewed, and I would be immediately fired if anyone complained about me."

— *Steven Magee, author of Toxic Electricity, Toxic Health, Toxic Light, Health Forensics*

Sound at all familiar? You're not alone. Everybody gets fired.

When big time Hired Gun, Lee Iacocca, published his autobiography, *Newsweek* magazine led its review of the book by quoting the first few pages:

"'On July 13, 1978, I was fired. I had been president of Ford for eight years and a Ford employee for 32. It was gut-wrenching. 'From his spacious suite atop World Headquarters, attended by white-coated servants, he was exiled to 'Siberia,' a warehouse cubicle in the farthest corner of Henry Ford's kingdom. 'Don't get mad,' his wife, Mary reminded him. 'Get even.' Iacocca went to Chrysler, and the rest was history."

Then, after he twice saved Chrysler from bankruptcy as its chairman, the Chrysler board forced him to retire. What did he do? He launched Iacocca Capital Partners in Los Angeles, joined the board of Kirk Kerkorian's MGM Grand in Las Vegas, and worked with Native Americans to build casinos on their tribal lands.

In the world of automobile manufacturing, there aren't many luminaries as big as Lee Iacocca, yet he was fired twice after producing outstanding results in his jobs. Likewise, in the world of television, there weren't many automobile luminaries as big as Jeremy Clarkson and his crew at the BBC program, *Top Gear.*

350 Million Viewers Per Episode - Fired

Motoring is not the same without Clarkson and his cohosts, Richard Hammond and James May. They were controversial, humorous, outspoken, and just plain fun.

The producers constantly placed them in life-challenging situations. Each week, they drove and critiqued expensive cars all over the world before a global audience of 350 million viewers in 214 territories. CBS's 60 Minutes called the show "a billion dollar global goldmine for the BBC." (By comparison, national network TV shows in the US get excited if they top eight million; the top-rated sitcom, *Big Bang Theory,* tops out around 18 million.)

When a *Top Gear* producer fouled up and failed to provide hot food available for the lead host after a long day of grueling driving stunts, Clarkson punched him, and his contract was not renewed. I do not envy the BBC's CEO, Lord Tony Hall, having to make a decision that resulted in the loss of millions of viewers.

When you own the opera house, you put up with the prima donnas. You don't have to put up with the stage hands, or the dress extras, but the prima donnas fill the seats in the opera halls.

— **Law of the Hired Gun with gratitude to Joe Charbonneau**

Fast forward to 2016. Jeremy Clarkson and *The Grand Tour* open the very first program on Amazon Prime with the Hothouse Flowers' version of Johnny Nash's popular song, "I Can See Clearly Now." Jeremy Clarkson is shown handing his office keys to an attendant in front of the BBC building before walking off into a rainy London day.

As this international celebrity rides away in a taxi, audio clips from various radio shows announce his sacking. We hear the announcement by BBC's CEO, Lord Tony Hall, that Clarkson's contract is not to be renewed. (His reported annual salary = GBP $10 million.) The cab drops him off at London Heathrow Airport.

Clarkson boards a plane for Los Angeles, and the music picks up its pace when he arrives at LAX and picks up a blue 725-horsepower, supercharged Galpin Fisker Ford Mustang *Rocket*.

As he roars down the sunlit highway, two other Mustangs fall in behind him, his former Top Gear cohosts, May in a red one and Hammond in white. Suddenly, they're driving across the California desert, supported by an enormous cast of exotic cars that kick up all manner of dust storms behind them, including a Dodge Challenger Hellcat, Lamborghini Aventador SV, Rolls Royce Ascot Tourer, the iHeart Music custom chariot, and a Plymouth Road Runner from *The Fast and Furious*.

The three Mustangs roll up to a large stage in the middle of nowhere USA to the rousing welcome of thousands of fans and the Hothouse Flowers on stage. After a Breitling Jet Team of eight Aero Albatrosses performs a dramatic fly-by overhead, the three presenters are introduced to the crowd.

Jeremy Clarkson:

That was the Hothouse Flowers! And look what we have here! He was FIRED by *Car* magazine, FIRED by *Autocar* magazine, FIRED by Scotland on Sunday, and somehow he managed to get FIRED by a Volvo dealership, probably for driving too slowly, ladies and gentlemen—James May! (Huge ovation).

James May:

Thank you, thank you, you're very kind. And ladies and gentlemen, you probably can't see him from the back but I assure you he is here! He was FIRED by Radio York, FIRED by Radio Leeds, and FIRED by Radio Lancashire! It's Richard Hammond! (Huge ovation).

Richard Hammond:

Thank you! And over here, he's basically a shaved ape in a shirt, and he technically is the only one of us never to be FIRED by anyone. It's Jeremy Clarkson!

Jeremy Clarkson:

Thank you so much! And the good thing is, it's very unlikely I'm going to be FIRED now because we're on the internet!

The crowd goes wild.

That's the way to handle getting fired.

Be proud that you got whacked. Beyond something like punching a producer, you normally get fired for only one of two reasons: 1) you're incompetent at your job, or 2) you're superlative at it to the extent you make others envious and fearful. I'm going to take a wild guess that because you're reading this, you are the latter.

If you can go online to Amazon Prime, find *The Grand Tour* show on their original programming list and watch this four-minute opening sequence of the Season 1/Episode 1 program. I highly recommend it.

Everybody gets FIRED. It isn't the firing that matters, but the future that opens up before you.

— Law of the Hired Gun

Lazarus - II

Early one Monday morning, I sit at our sales admin assistant's desk while I catch up on my mail and messages. I'm far from happy, actually a bit depressed as I sift through the sales team's suspension file folders for mine. I'm in no hurry.

One of my best friends is in our manager's office 10 feet away, ostensibly getting fired.

When he missed work Friday without calling the office, our Junior Suit openly blustered that it's the end of the line for him when he comes back Monday morning. Lazarus is not only a phenomenal sales rep but also just as phenomenal a friend. We work well together, and I don't look forward to this ending of our sales shenanigans or to breaking in some new replacement rep directly across from my Boof.

If anyone is the Sundance Kid of Sales, it's Lazarus. If he needs to get a deal in by the end of the day with nothing showing in his pipeline, he finds one, works it, sells it, and closes it that day. Just to emphasize this point, this is when we are selling distance learning TV subscriptions for between $15,000/year to $60,000/year in 2018 terms. The normal sales cycle is about 90 days. For example, it took me over two years to close my deal with the USAF.

As much as I hate and protest requirements of PROCESS, I probably follow a process more than most reps. It's just that it's my own process, developed through trials of fire by myself and based on actions that repeatedly result in closed deals.

It doesn't include spreadsheets, reports, meetings, or other impediments to doing the work that gets deals done. I always have an accurate idea of how many deals are in position to close each month with my own Hot List. But on those occasions when one or two sure things I've bet on pull up lame, and I need an unaccounted deal to come in quickly, my best recourse is to pray to St. Expedite.

Lazarus works the deals just like the rest of us, but he also has that incredible ability to pull a rabbit out of his hat pretty much every time he needs one. Our Junior Suit who's firing him is an OK guy; we get along fine. He just has it in his head that he's fed up with our collection of 10 iconoclastic sales reps and has his heart set on making an example. I fear he's making a sizable mistake if he terminates one of his consistent top producers, when one mature discussion and attitude adjustment meeting will do the job.

I look up when the Junior Suit's office door opens. Lazarus looks over at me as he walks by and says, "Ha! Smoked 'im!"

We take a break to the coffee room, and I ask for details. Lazarus replies, "Oh, he was chapping me about missing last Friday when I went to LA and said he was going to fire me."

"What happened?"

"I told him not to threaten me with my job; it pisses me off."

And that's it. Lazarus comes back to life, thus his nickname. Later, they try to fire him again. And he survives again. We upgrade his nickname a notch, to Lazarus II.

Firing Lesson #1: It May Not Actually Happen

You might be able to pull a Lazarus and talk the Suit out of it if you want to. I talk a lot about getting whacked in sales, and I've lost a number of sales jobs I've really liked, but those were almost all cases where I left or the companies closed, not cases of being terminated. There are only two cases where I was fired and regretted leaving the company. Another time it was a blessing in disguise.

You can protest for wrongful termination and file a lawsuit. If you do, make sure you have an iron-clad case. Today when companies fire someone, it is not unlike getting raided by the Department of Justice. You're focused on doing your job so you don't pick up on the telltale signs around you, while the Suits have all the time in the world to build and document their case against you. Thus, you get caught by surprise. It's all part of their plan. You walk into work one day, get called into an office, and BLAM! you're shot.

If you contest it, make sure you have all your facts in order, call a meeting with the person who whacked you, and bring in your attorneys. Get the biggest Great White Shark law firm you can find and turn them loose to chew on your former Suit. If nothing else, you'll have the satisfaction of watching the Junior Suit squirm. At best, you might get reinstated or come out with a pretty good severance package beyond what was offered. At this point, what do you have to lose?

Firing Lesson #2: They May Be Doing You a Favor

More than likely, you're set free from the shackles of micro-management at your Mature Market company. Now you can go find another Genesis enterprise at which you can achieve. If you are the top producer and get whacked because your success makes other people envious, it's time for you to get out anyway. You just got bushwhacked. Next time you'll know better and saddle up on your own terms.

When I got whacked from my inside sales job worth the 2018 equivalent of $300,000 a year, the Geek-Speak Suit said, "Um, OK, um, we have met, and, um, it is, um, management's decision that in the future direction of the company, um, you are no longer part of that direction. Um, OK." *Beep! Whirrrr... Bzzzzzzzzzz!*

Spectre

An interesting parallel occurs in the James Bond movie, *Spectre,* in which a dangerous internal threat is revealed within British Intelligence. Max Denbigh, the new internal King of Geek-Speak (sarcastically referred to as "C" by both Bond and M) believes that human espionage is archaic due to the technological advent of drones and satellites. That's like a lot of sales guru geeks today when they announce that sales is dead, and we just need to take orders online for everything all day.

C announces his crowning achievement when he informs M that he's snaked around behind the scenes to arrange the shut-down of the entire Double-0 section of the British Secret Service. C is a big believer in globalist one-world nonsense and is arranging for nations to share their intelligence gathering data via technology.

How similar is this conversation in *Spectre* from your company's **C**IO persuading your suits to close down the entire sales department because everything can now be bought and sold online?

C:
Nine Eyes is now officially sanctioned. The new system goes live in less than 72 hours. It's a major step forward. Global intelligence cooperation changes everything.

M:
As you said before.

C:
Look. They've asked me to head the new committee.

M:
Yes? And?

C:
And I should tell you I've spoken with the Home Secretary. And in light of the new information I've given him, he's decided to close down the Double-0 program with immediate effect.

M:
You don't know what you're doing.

C:
Our new CRM system, *G.O.D.* is now officially sanctioned. The new system goes live in less than 72 hours. It's a major step forward. Data, metrics, and spreadsheets change everything about sales.

M:
As you said before.

C:
Look. They've asked me to head the restructuring.

M:
Yes? And?

C:
And I should tell you I've spoken with our COO and CFO. And in light of the new information I've given them, they've decided to close down the sales department with immediate effect.

M:
You don't know what you're doing.

C:
It's not personal. It's the future. And...you're not.

M:
You're a cocky little bastard, aren't you?

C:
I'll take that as a compliment.

M:
I wouldn't. This isn't over yet.

C:
It's not personal. It's the future.
And...you're not.

M:
You're a cocky little bastard, aren't you?

C:
I'll take that as a compliment.

M:
I wouldn't. This isn't over yet.

I have to admit, the Geek-Speak Suit who whacked me from my $300,000-a-year job did me a favor. Under his lack of leadership, the company was going straight downhill while I was off in "a different direction" doing extremely well. But I might have ended up hanging around too long as my income dwindled with the rest of the company's revenues.

This immediately forced me to open the door for a big move forward in my sales career. At the time, I observed the growing high-tech trend in sales and wondered if I had the ability to climb into that arena. Getting fired forced me to make that adjustment, an adjustment that became the direction of the next 20 years of my sales career.

Firing Lesson #3: Have a Party!

Yes, definitely. Really. This isn't just a war story from a sales guy. This isn't just some sunshine pump fluff; this is the best thing you can do for yourself. Throw a party immediately, the same day you get whacked. If you're reading this a few days or weeks later, that's OK, have it as soon as possible. The point is, celebrate your new beginning!

Strike while the iron is hot. Immediately get word back to your best friends at your former office. Tell them you're throwing a party at your place (or at your bar) that night to celebrate the fact that *"Pheeeeonnnh! I'm outta here!"* Get word out to your social spheres, get word out to everyone. *Open bar!* On me! *Tonight!*

It's OK to tell them you would really like for them to be there in support. They know you just took a bullet. Besides, they're probably just a little bit envious of you. You no longer have to endure the conga line dance numbers put on by *Armani and the Suits*. Here's a little email template you can use to get started:

EMAIL: Subject: *"I just got Fired! Help me celebrate!"* Content: *"Swing by tonight to help me celebrate my new direction!" (details)* and *"Please Forward."* Wouldn't you go to that party if it was a friend of yours? (With an open bar?)

Here's what happens. At the apex of the evening, you blast out the song by Johnny Paycheck, *"Take This Job and Shove It!"* In the middle of your group, you pop the cork on your bottle of champagne. Everybody cheers!

The action alone signifies celebration, and the sound is that of a starting gun for the next leg of your race. Instead of feeling down in the dumps, you're on top of the world. You're partying with your closest friends and acquaintances.

They all support you and volunteer to help in various ways. They admire your positive attitude. The word gets out that you're available. People know how good you are; the message just needs to land on ears that belong to someone who needs a top-tier sales rep.

Plus, filling out little boxes in *G.O.D.* and the day-to-day stress of your old job is gone. Let them worry about those things now. Play tonight. You can sleep in tomorrow!

Be sure to check your messages the very next morning. The American business jungle lives on supply and demand. Reps of your quality and experience are in short supply, and demand is high. You'll probably have a voicemail from someone who heard you're suddenly available and needs sales help. I'm not kidding; it's happened to me twice.

Firing Lesson #4: Take the High Road

Bashing your former employer—or anybody for that matter—only makes you look small. You may dislike them or you may hate their guts and want to drag them naked across a field of broken glass but keep it to yourself. Your colleagues at work already know the score. Your friends know the score as well.

As a matter of fact, if the Suit who fired you finds out about your party and has the *cojones* to show up at your door, invite him in. Who knows? He might have been ordered by some Senior Suit to fire you. That happened to me, too. Or, he might just be a jerk. Either way, exercising grace rarely counts against you and always comes back to you in a good way.

> **"You're never wrong when you do the right thing."**
>
> — *Mark Twain*

Firing Lesson #5: Create Your Big Book of You

You sell everything else well; it's time to sell yourself. Go far beyond what other people show when they interview for a new position. Everybody in the world has a resume, and so do you. Make sure it's as tight and exciting to read as possible.

But if you don't already have one, create a supplemental Big Book of You. The Suit that interviews you sees a hundred resumes that proclaim "increased revenue," "grew my sales territory," or "won the company award for top producer four years in a row."

Please don't misunderstand me, you need to announce these things as well. But those are just the beginning, merely the headlines. You want to go deeper than that, and you should. You have a lot more to offer, and you can document your achievements.

Put together an attractive business-oriented, three-ring binder with index tabs that divide sections of pertinent documentation about you. Here are some ideas for your sections: Your bio; testimonial letters from clients, colleagues, Suits; congratulatory internal memos; year-end paychecks; commission checks; **copies of big checks or payments from clients**; and photos of you winning awards. Share everything that is impressive about you. Don't just say it. Show it.

This separates you from the competition. Anybody can talk about all the wonderful things they claim to have achieved. Anybody can talk the talk; show that you walk the walk.

At some point, every interview eventually gets to That Point. You're a top-tier sales rep. You can read the momentum and timing. You sense it. When the time is right, let the interviewer know you brought along some supplemental material you thought they would be interested in seeing. It's kind of like waiting for everyone else to turn over their hands in a poker game while you patiently and confidently wait to show your cards last because you're the one holding a straight flush.

When you show them **your big payment checks from your biggest clients**, your testimonial letters from within your company and from your clients, and photos of you winning your company's Top Producer of the Year award, you get their attention. This act alone demonstrates the professionalism of a top-tier player, and they don't forget you.

DO NOT LEAVE YOUR BOOK BEHIND

You will never see it again. Suits will confiscate and appropriate it to use as a model when building their own books. Or the interviewer will keep it to job block you.

No matter what, hold onto your book. It's the product of a lot of hard work. If they really want to keep something to review, leave a thumb drive of its contents or let them make copies while you're there. Again, <u>never</u> give up your book. Do not leave it behind to pick up later. It will disappear. I guarantee it.

Firing Lesson #6: Start Your Own Business

This might be exactly the right time for you to start your own business. That was the case when I founded my little direct mail company.

Alternatively, a good steady-paying job selling for an innovative operation may be exactly what you need. That was the case when I had to close down the direct mail company after we grew through three pretty good years.

Opening a shop was Roy's move after our company rewarded him for his superlative efforts by firing him on his birthday. Roy's magic words were just a bit more powerful than Mary Iacocca's. He told the Suits, "I'm not going to get mad. I'm going to get even. And it's going to cost you millions."

Within three months, he contracted our former operation's major local client to move to his new company at the first available moment, obtained millions in vulture capitalist financing, and signed for the construction of a new 70,000-square-foot building. And he took the entire A-Team with him.

Similarly, Bernard Marcus was 49 years old as CEO of Handy Dan hardware stores and Arthur Blank was 36 as vice president of finance when both were fired in 1978 as part of an internal power struggle. What did they do? They founded Home Depot in Atlanta, Georgia. Their current net worth, according to *Forbes*: Bernard Marcus, $3.3 billion. Arthur Blank, $4 billion.

So What?

What's the FIRST THING to do if you get fired? Why not access and listen to the **Hired Gun Playlist** on our website at **HiredGun.us**? Listen to it in your car as you drive away and put that place in your rearview mirror.

The reason the play list is there is *you*—and it's *FREE!* The songs are selected to help reassure you about who you are as a Hired Gun sales rep, and they're available to help provide a little bit of entertaining and uplifting emotional support when you need it most.

You may identify with the overall theme of these popular musical pieces when you are forced to deal with the shenanigans of people who seek to control you, squeeze you into a box of conformity, steal from you, undermine your job, and want you out of there because your excellence makes them feel inadequate with themselves.

Pump up the volume and redeem yourself! *Let's Party!*

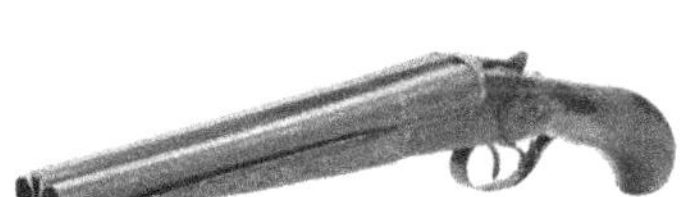

Levity Break

A company's board believes it's time for an internal shake-up and hires a new CEO.

The new executive decides to make an example out of its slackers.

On a highly visible tour of the facilities, the CEO notices a guy leaning against a wall, checking his phone.

The CEO walks up to the guy and asks, "How much do you get paid every week?"

The young guy shrugs, looks at him, and replies, "$300 a week. Why?"

The CEO hands the guy $300 cash and bellows so all his employees can hear, "Here's a week's pay, now GET OUT and don't come back!"

Feeling pretty good about his first example, the CEO looks around and asks, "What did that goof-off do around here, anyway?"

One of the workers mutters, "Pizza delivery guy."

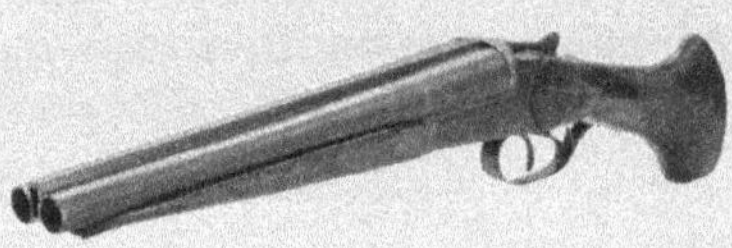

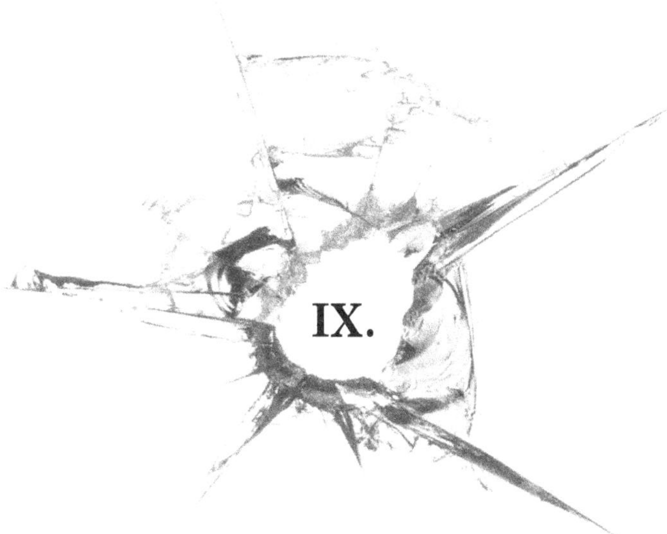

IX.

Geek-Speak — The New! Improved! *Esperanto!*

In which we examine the pretentious, contrived, manufactured, and tortured language commonly used throughout today's business world

The Encyclopedia Britannica defines *Esperanto* as "an artificial language" devised in 1887 by Ludwig Lazarus Zamenhof, a Polish eye doctor, to be an international second language. Today's corporate geek jargon can be defined the same way: "an artificial language."

Please remember three premises:

1. The Real Deal is, human nature does not change.

2. The Real Deal is, human beings cause everything to happen in business and commerce.

3. The *Real* Deal is, I only deal with the *Real* Deal. (i.e. not "artificial language.")

Human beings are behind everything; not robots, not spreadsheets, not computer gadgets or online widgets. I couldn't care less about the trendy business books o' the month that get spit out every Q1 or Q2 by alleged business or sales gurus in their ivory towers.

What's interesting is how quickly these disquisitions are quietly shelved and forgotten upon the launch of the next book or symposium that announces newer, manufactured corporate geek jargon and pretentious theory. Sure, they sound timely and jazzy, and make great dinner conversation for Suits; sure, they create ways to sell books. But nobody remembers them five years later.

FOR EXAMPLE:

Do you remember the Japanese Business Superiority craze in **the '80s**? Japanese business principles. Japanese business practices. Japanese business economics. Japanese this, Japanese that, and Japanese everything else. The *zeitgeist* held that the Japanese knew more than anyone else in the world about how to create and build successful businesses. And that's all we heard about for a decade. The '80s movies, *Black Rain* and *Rising Sun,* come to mind. Where is all that now? *Shinda.*

When email technology soared in popularity in **the '90s**, it was all about SPAM. You could legally rent a list, including launch and delivery, and blast an email ad to more than one million names for about 70 bucks. I know because I did that with "Deathofthe.com," a fun little novella I wrote as an eBook.

"You've got mail" was such a popular phrase that it became the title of a popular movie with Tom Hanks and Meg Ryan. Mick Jagger's voice announced the phrase whenever an email magically popped into my inbox. "Open rates" and "click through rates" also were hot hip marketing concepts and terms. Where are they now? They're so commonplace we don't even consider them. I've got a popular '80s phrase for the techie linguists: "where's the beef?"

A little later in **the Oughts**, more conscientious marketing practices replaced SPAM with "permission-based marketing." Is that term still bandied about? Of course not. It was absorbed into the standard set of operational values for mainstream email and social media marketing campaigns and became quickly *passé.* Another trendy phrase was "burn rate," used to reference how fast a company was blowing through its financial reserves. This term reached its zenith right at the dot-com crash of 2001.

Today, the talking head pundits discuss how the 2017 holiday season set sales records because of the strongest online shopping, ever. This, they claim, is due to the methods that marketers employ to target prospective buyers using **digital media + social media + service wave analytics**. Basically, online consumers are besieged by ubiquitous online ads triggered through this contrived artificial intelligence that recalls their recent online searches or purchases.

In its *Fourth Annual State of Marketing* report published in 2017, Salesforce Research found "about half (51 percent) of marketing leaders are already using AI, with more than a quarter planning to pilot it in the next two years."

Today's newest corporate geek phrase is "**customer experience marketing,**" which Salesforce Research says marketing leaders are now "battling" over.

"Customer experience is central to their go-to market strategy, in how they aim to win new customers, and in how they're keeping current making sure the customer has a positive experience when companies market to them," the report read. This can be anything from positive in-store customer service and finding physical store locations online via a map search to seeing a marketer's ads on social feeds like Instagram or Facebook.

Please indulge me. This is, of course, a great concept but isn't this the way it should be, anyway? Should it be necessary to make such a big deal about treating customers like they're important and valuable as if that's something new? Marshall Field used "customer experience marketing" to build his eponymous retail department store powerhouse (since purchased by Macy's) more than a century ago.

In a September 2018 article in *Forbes*, "A Global View Of 'The Customer is Always Right,'" author and "customer experience futurist" Blake Morgan writes:

> The customer is always right is a phrase pioneered by Harry Gordon Selfridge, John Wanamaker, and Marshall Field. These men were successful retailers and learned early in their careers that the success of their stores depended on the happiness of their customers...

> They didn't actually intend the phrase to mean that the customer was in the right in every situation. Instead, it was a signal that customers were special. Staff were instructed to treat customers as if they were always right, even if it was obvious they weren't. The change in mindset was a radical shift to how customers were used to being treated, and people flocked to these department stores.

Of course, new ideas and sales techniques need to emerge to deal with new competition in the marketplace. We constantly need to adapt to changes brought about by technological innovations that alter how we communicate in person and *en masse.* A competitive business needs to stay at the forefront of these new opportunities to gain eyeball time with prospective buyers. Make no mistake, I really like most of these advancements in communication media.

But then I watch some guy prance around on stage as he flashes a big over-enthusiastic smile and pontificates to his audience like he's Eric Cartman in *South Park.* He reveals an exciting concept like "customer experience marketing." I think, *"Whatever. I'm here for knowledge transfer and new information. Let's see what he's got."* Before an adoring throng of followers that eagerly awaits his announcement of The Next Big Thing, I hear the equivalent of:

"I'm smart. I'm cool, and here are some new trendy contrived Geek Speak Esperanto cool sounding tech terms that you don't know yet because I just made them up."

Mm-hmm. "Thanks for the extra large with sausage and pepperoni. Here's your tip."

By contrast, here's a different tip, and some simple language to help illustrate better the *New! Improved!* hot, hip concept of **customer experience marketing,** as reported several years ago by InsightsForAnalytics.com and BarterCard.com.au:

WHY CUSTOMERS LEAVE
1) 1 percent die
2) 3 percent move away
3) 5 percent find other relationships
4) 9 percent are persuaded to go to a competitor
5) 14 percent are dissatisfied with your product or service
6) 68 percent leave because of a perceived attitude of indifference shown by an employee

— **Law of the Hired Gun**

Or, consider this from a short article published in July 2014 in the *Dallas Morning News*:

> "In the mid 1960s a 30-year-old mom walked into the Dallas Lincoln dealership and said that her small company had a great year, and to treat herself she wanted to buy the black Lincoln Town Car that was in the showroom. The salesman put his arm around her shoulder and walked her to the door and said, "When your husband gets off work today, have him come by and I'll work a car deal with him, meanwhile we're busy here."
>
> At the Dallas Cadillac dealership, they were interested and showed her a car that Elvis Presley had influenced Cadillac to offer, a dusty pink.... She bought it and drove back to the office.... A few years later they decided to make a new pink Cadillac the grand award for their top sales ladies.
>
> As of today, that small Dallas company has bought over 22,000 pink Cadillacs and not a single Lincoln Town Car. And to think, the pink Cadillac became their icon...
>
> ...the sales guy at the Lincoln dealership? He stayed there until he retired but was always referred to as, "Bob, the guy that threw Mary Kay (Cosmetics) out the door."

The Hired Gun's 10-10-10 Rule

It takes $10,000 to get a new customer.
It takes 10 seconds to lose them.
It takes 10 years to get them back.

Just Sell

I got a call from a friend who worked next to me during the satellite TV network sales era. We enjoyed a fun standing bet that whomever of us produced the highest revenue each month bought a steak dinner for the other guy. And we busted our butts for those steaks.

He was about to start a new position selling high-tech software solutions and knew that I recently enjoyed several good years selling for a software development company. Steve wanted to know if I had any pointers that could help him get off to a good start in high-tech sales.

"Yes, there's definitely one thing I'll tell you," I said. "You're going to get in there with a bunch of guys, all of you selling a new business software solution. They're all there because they have some kind of background in high tech. I'm going to take a wild guess that you're like me in my first high-tech sales job, and they hired you because you have a track record of success in sales."

I went on, "Here's what's going to happen. You're not going to know much about the deep technical ins-and-outs of your products when you start. You're going to do what you know how to do: Get on the phone, make calls, send emails, and follow up. Learn as much as you can as fast as you can, ask questions, and do all the things that you and I accept as normal new-guy sales behavior."

"Then, you watch," I said. "The other guys won't make calls, and they won't directly contact 20 prospects a day like you will. But they'll impress each other around the office with techie corporate geek jargon to show how much they think they know about high tech. And they'll do this with you, too. They want to make you feel inadequate because you're just some sales guy the company brought in while they're techies!"

Technology — everybody's an expert and nobody knows squat.

— Law of the Hired Gun with gratitude to James Montgomery

I went on, "In a few months after you've closed a bunch of deals and the other guys have big goose eggs on the board, they won't be around anymore, and you'll become the guy who knows the correct, appropriate corporate geek terms to use, and when to use them. You're a sharp salesman; you learn fast and you have a lifetime of successful sales behavior. So, don't let the pinheads get you down. In the end, you'll be there, and they'll be gone.

"My advice to you? In a nutshell, just sell."

About six months later, I ran into Steve and his girlfriend one night. He said, "Hey, you know all that stuff you told me about what would happen when I started at my new company? You were exactly right! Exactly! Just a bunch of high-tech gossip all the time and no real work done, and I just tried to get in there and sell, and it worked out just the way you said."

Steve is now a Vice President for SAP.

Don't let a bunch of geek-speak phonies make you feel inadequate. They're the ones who feel inadequate; that's why they're spouting off all the stuff they pretend to know. Because they know they can't sell.

Now, who *can* sell? The Boss. And The Boss is the person least likely to be interested in corporate geek jargon. Maybe not among his peers over cocktails but within The Boss's own ranks, the Suits know to get to the point or they learn quickly.

"TCB" - Taking Care of Business

I'm a kid watching a movie, and it will profoundly influence the direction of my life. Is it an epic like *Ben-Hur?* An avant-garde production like *On the Waterfront?* An American classic like *Who's Afraid of Virginia Woolf? 2001: A Space Odyssey? Citizen Kane, Casablanca,* or *It's a Wonderful Life?*

No, it's *Clambake.* Featuring Elvis Presley.

To this highly impressionable, red-blooded adolescent, it wasn't the girls, girls, girls, or cool cars or music that caught my attention. It was Elvis' dad in the movie—an oilman who also is The Boss and, to me, a far more interesting character. As the story develops, the movie cuts to a scene in his swanky Petroleum Club-esque penthouse office. Half a dozen navy blue Suits seated around a conference table pitch a deal to The Boss, who sits at his desk with his administrative assistant. He props his feet up and polishes one of his cowboy boots as he smokes a cigar.

What follows is a succinct lesson in how not to pitch The Boss with corporate geek jargon.

SUIT:
As Director of Research and Development, it is a function of my position to explore the advantages of diversification. However, acquisition for the sake of diversification is not a profitable undertaking. Therefore, it is my strong recommendation that we accept Allied Chemical's generous offer and turn over all completed and incomplete experiments, formulas, and data on our ill-fated hunt for glycol-oxooctanoic-phosphate.

BOSS:
You mean "GOOP?"

SUIT:
Yes, sir. That's—what I mean.

BOSS:
Well if that's what you mean, say it. Don't go confusing me!

SUIT:
Yes, sir! Uh, no, sir!

Believe me, the last person who wants to sit in a meeting and listen to a bunch of corporate geek jargon is The Boss. But before you can pitch your deal to The Boss, you need to nail that interview to win your new sales position.

How to Ace Your High-Tech Sales Job Interview

So, you have a job interview with a high-tech company for an account executive position?

Numerous blogs, articles, videos, websites, and coaches exist that provide tips to help prepare for a successful interview with everything from what to eat the previous night to what pen and color ink to use in the meeting.

Here are a couple of in-depth, heavily researched, comprehensive bottom-line tips about interviewing for that high-tech sales position from your friendly neighborhood Hired Gun.

First, sell this interviewer the same way you'd sell any company executive at a prospective customer's office.

Second, name drop several of today's hottest, hippest sounding techie geek-jargon terms. You don't really have to know what they mean. If necessary, just say you're familiar with them and learning more about their application in current *"BI" (Business Intelligence)*. Some examples:

- Virtual Assistants
- Pattern BI
- Humanized Big Data
- Informed Data Lake
- Digital Twin
- Augmented Analytics
- Accessible BI
- Artificial Intelligence (AI)
- Internet of Things
- Blockchain Technology
- Digital Detox/Digital Productivity
- Microservices/Microservice Architecture
- Serverless Architecture
- Mobile First
- Dark Data
- Actionable Analytics/Self-Service Analytics

Pick out a couple of terms you like, and jumble them together:

"I don't know why so many people are concerned about AI and the Internet of Things. Over half of current marketing companies use AI already, and it's going to increase another 25 percent or more in a few years. And the Internet of Things is just everything. I mean, with last year's huge sales records for Black Friday and Cyber Monday, you have growing Mobile First technology combined with shoppers' Actionable Analytics. Combine that with the future direction of Blockchain Technology, and you can see the need to stay on the cutting edge of all this stuff."

What did you just say? Not a damn thing. But it sounds good, doesn't it?

And, last but not least, here's my #3 tip: Do the Deal.

The Retro-Turbo-Micro-Encabulator

For advanced work in the field of corporate geek jargon, you might enjoy studying up on the Turbo-encabulator. Rebecca Linke, Senior Associate Editor for Computerworld wrote an op-ed on August 27, 2013 that detailed the history of this sensible sounding gibberish. This marvelous invention spoof first appeared in 1944 when a paper by student John Hellins Quick, "The Turbo-Encabulator in History," was printed in the *British Institution of Electrical Engineers Student's Quarterly Journal.* In 1946, the paper was reprinted Stateside in the *Arthur D. Little Industrial Bulletin. Time* magazine followed suit in April 1946, reprinting the article as "For Nofer Trunions," and the rest is history.

On YouTube today, you can see the first known video made about the Retro-encabulator in 1977 by Rockwell Automotive. More recently, it reemerged as the Micro Encabulator in another spoof video on YouTube made by PATH Industries in Philadelphia.

For your entertainment, I recommend checking out one or two of these for a practical history lesson in quality Geek Speak. Here's an excerpt from the Rockwell Automotive video:

> "The original machine had a base plate of preformulated Amulite surmounted by a malleable logarithmic casing in such a way that the two sperving bearings were in a direct line with the panometric fam. The latter consisted simply of six hydrocoptic marzelvanes, so fitted to the ablofascient lunar waneshaft that side fumbling

> was effectively prevented. The main winding was of the Lotus Ode Delta type placed in panendermic semi-boloid slots of the stator, every seventh conductor being connected by a nonreversible tremi pipe connected to the differential girdle spring on the up-end of the grammeters..."

Anybody can do it. And everybody knows it. But The Wizard of Oz and the Suits like to think their stilted verbal retroencabulatorisms impress other people, especially other Suits, while everyone else is having a good laugh. That's why, when an email memo written in really good hyperbolic geek-speak jargon hits your inboxes, you look around to observe the windows of your colleagues' souls.

First, their eyes roll in disbelief at yet another book-length text of geek speak.

Second, their eyes glaze over as they spend hours trying to decipher what is being said.

Finally, they get sleepy, and your colleagues drift off with visions of *The Sorcerer's Apprentice* delivering mountains of geek-speak emails dancing in their heads.

Don't pay attention to what people say; watch what they do. It tells you who they are.

— Law of the Hired Gun with gratitude to Joe Charbonneau

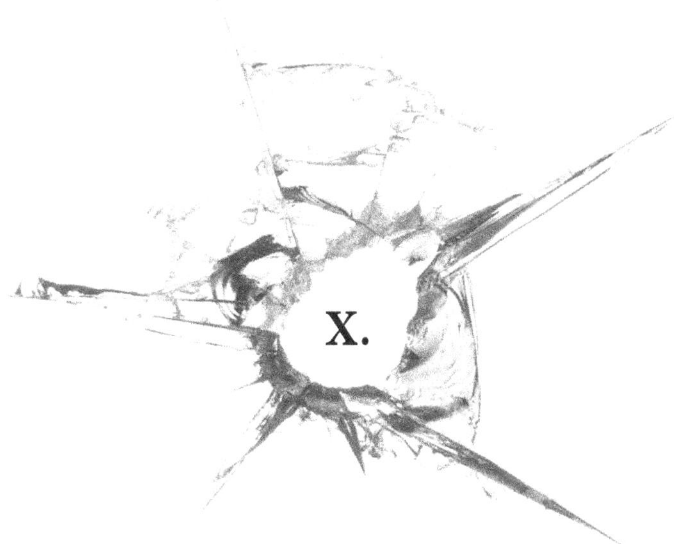

Your Single Greatest Asset

In which you perform one task that automatically places you in the top 3 percent of people in our society

Out of the night that covers me,
Black as the pit from pole to pole,
I thank whatever gods may be
For my unconquerable soul.

In the fell clutch of circumstance
I have not winced nor cried aloud.
Under the bludgeonings of chance
My head is bloody, but unbowed.

Beyond this place of wrath and tears
Looms but the Horror of the shade,
And yet the menace of the years
Finds and shall find me unafraid.

It matters not how strait the gate,
How charged with punishments the scroll,
I am the master of my fate,
I am the captain of my soul.

INVICTUS
William Ernest Henley

Simply put, your single greatest asset is You.

The problem is, many of us have never been directly exposed to the fact that our assessment of our personal value determines everything that happens to us in our life.

Your self-image is the driving force for everything that you do and everything that happens to you, for better or worse. It's a mental picture of yourself that you carry around with you every day of your life. If you want to truly tap into and exploit your greatest asset, it is first essential that you know everything there is to know about that person in your mental picture.

Every day, you go out and take that picture of yourself into the marketplace. How you see yourself in that picture, how well you leverage that self-image, determines everything else in your life: How you create new beginnings, how you respond to opportunities, how you deal with people, what you do for a living, where you go every day, where you live, where your kids go to school, the car you drive, and the people with whom you associate. These all come down to the thoughts that occupy your mind about who you are, and then, what you do.

If you want to change something about your life, change the thoughts that occupy your mind.

— **Law of the Hired Gun**

You may be familiar with Proverbs 23:7: "As a man thinketh in his heart, so is he."

All our lives, we've also heard versions of the ancient Greek aphorism from the Delphi maxims, "**Know thyself.**" Fine, everybody tells us to know ourselves. Excellent.

One Question: has anybody ever shown you *how?*

In the era of primitive mainframe computers, there was a popular axiom called, "GIGO." Dictionary.com defines the term as "a rule of thumb stating that when faulty data are fed into a computer, the information that emerges is also faulty." The British Dictionary definition is more succinct: "garbage in—garbage out." If a computer has garbage programmed into it, it will produce garbage coming out of it. Humans are the same. If our minds accept garbage, that is what comes out.

It's much like food. If the only nourishment we provide our bodies is crummy food, our bodies only have that to draw from, and produce crummy results. In October 2017, a National Center for Health Statistics report asked, "What was the prevalence of obesity in adults in 2015-2016? The prevalence of obesity among US adults was 39.8 percent (crude)."

What is crummy food? For example, just about everything you see advertised on TV from frozen dinners to donuts and fast food burgers—all with prices that end in 0.99. It's cheap to screw yourself up. Cheap foods infused with pesticides, preservatives, and sugars lead to weight gain, diabetes, heart problems, cancers, the list goes on. Simple question: if it was *really* good food and good for you, would they need to push it on you via multibillion-dollar saturation ad campaigns?

Good food is not expensive; bad food is cheap.

— **Law of the Hired Gun**

Conversely, when you put Real Food into your body, good things result: Lower blood pressure, lower body fat, better quality skin and hair, a clearer mind, the list goes on. If you want to improve your physical health, try eating only Real Food.

Similarly, if you want to improve your mental health, change what you put into your mind every day. When you put positive, good thoughts into your mind, it responds exactly the same way. This isn't theoretical physics; it's simple common sense.

Then Why Don't We Do It?

The difficulty with putting positive concepts into our own minds manifests itself daily across America. And for once, this is something that is truly not our fault. Negativity starts first thing in the morning and continues to plague us throughout the day and night, if we let it. We are so overrun by Crummy News that anything good has a hard time getting in.

Most people get up in the morning and turn on the TV or check their mobile device to watch the news. What's on? Alcohol, drugs, murder, rape, terrorism, theft, and war.

Then they go downstairs to have breakfast and read the morning newspaper in print or online. What's in it? Alcohol, drugs, murder, rape, terrorism, theft, and war.

Then they get in the car or on the train to commute to work and listen to the radio for more of the same: alcohol, drugs, murder, rape, terrorism, theft, and war.

Whenever I speak, I make sure to go to the local newsstand that morning to pick up that day's newspaper. When I get to this point in my presentation, I open it and read the headlines from the front page. I never have to check it in advance. They're always the same.

Farmers aren't going to farm anymore because bankers aren't banking anymore because stockbrokers are broke and the politicians are all crooked and we're all going to hell in a hand basket...

...electronically mainlined into our minds all day long every day at the rate of 4,615 images per minute.

It's called the 24-hour news cycle.

On April 2, 2018, Monmouth University released a poll that concluded 77 percent of Americans believe traditional media outlets report "fake news." So now we're worried about things that most of us think may very well not even be true in the first place?

After being inundated with bad news, people are supposed to trudge into the office to help other people? Now tell me, how are you going to help other people when you've filled your mind at the rate of 4,615 images per minute with disasters? Every day.

We can hardly avoid bad news even if we try. And then there's artificial intelligence, the same technology that knows your toilet paper preferences so it can push ads in front of your eyes, and also makes sure you see plenty of news, too.

Now, think about the reason why: Money. Media companies, like any other, rely on advertising sales revenues.

Clark Gable sums it up succinctly in the classic Doris Day rom-com, *Teacher's Pet.* As city editor Jim Gannon of *The Chronicle,* he compares a failed country newspaper to his mighty metropolitan daily:

GABLE:

Look at this. Published twice weekly...circulation 2,500...
one page of advertising...with no other sheet to give him competition.
That isn't a newspaper, it's a hobby!
You know, you may not believe it, but I'm interested in those kids you're teaching.
But in the name of Pulitzer, tell them the truth!
Tell them this is a business, a rough, tough, fighting, clawing business.
The Chronicle has a circulation of a half million.
Each copy sells for a dime and costs at least 10 cents to print.
We stay alive by advertising...the same as every other paper in this town...
and we battle each other for it.

The objective of the mass media is to fill air time or bits and bytes on your mobile device or computer with information they believe will entice you to read on. They want your eyes to be attracted to strategically placed advertisements that you can't avoid seeing. The goal is for you to get suckered in by their clickbait or by their telephone number—*now!*—and to goad you into spending $5.99 to eat their crummy food.

In August 2018, Google admitted that they installed location tracking software on our phones and that this enabled other apps, completely independent of Google, to also track our daily lives. Once they were caught, Google changed its policy to say, "This setting does not affect other location services on your device."

Facebook was also caught tracking us, as well as other tech companies.

George Orwell's classic book, *1984*, is becoming truer and truer but the latest version isn't driven by our government but by advertising dollars. By knowing where we are and where we're going, they can send us ads that anticipate our next location and can influence us to buy junk when we get there.

Who's Zooming Who?

On-air personalities tell you all about their purpose being to "inform the public," or "provide information services to the public," or "provide entertainment content to the public," or whatever FCC regulation the broadcast programs want to cite. The bottom line is, many of these radio talk show hosts, alleged TV journalists, anchor people, actors, and actresses owe their livelihoods to commercial advertising time sold by salespeople.

Without salespeople selling ad time to support their "content," they're out of business. *Shinda.* The point is, don't think of media personalities as demi-gods worthy of being in charge of the ideas that enter your mind. They aren't. They're sources of information about alcohol, drugs, murder, rape, terrorism, theft, and war supported by ad dollars. Stop willfully seeking out their bad news.

The best you can do is exercise control over what you choose to take in and when you choose to do it. I generally sequester my news to the end of the day and before lights out, with time for a good comedy afterward so I end the day with positive humorous thoughts. Don't leave it up to "them." Otherwise, your thoughts might get taken over by the next tech company that wants to not only track your travel patterns but also invade your mind.

Hired Gun Question: How long will it be until TPC (The Phone Company) develops the technology to put tiny chips in our brains so we can communicate telepathically with one another and have our thoughts tapped like phone lines? (You think this sounds ridiculous? It's the plot of the movie, *The President's Analyst,* made back in 1968.)

Choose to listen, read, and watch what *you* consciously select. Listen to your own music play lists. You made them because you know what you like to hear. Listen to positive and helpful audio books and podcasts. Instead of putting garbage in your mind, absorb information that's beneficial to you.

Positive Thought Replacement

PsychCentral.com posted an excellent article by Erika Krull in July 2016 titled, "Replacing Your Negative Thoughts." Here's some of what she says:

> When you **do something** that makes you feel more in control, you take the fuel out of your negative thoughts.... And now, you are starting to put better more encouraging thoughts into your mind.... These are starting to come more easily each day. Negative thoughts may still come at you.... They become easier to replace because your feelings are being driven by more positive thoughts.

For example, an excellent time to enter new positive thoughts in your mind is just before you go to sleep. Instead of watching the depressing local or national news before bed, watch a comedy and think new positive thoughts about who you are and what you do. When you wake, you will find it a lot easier to have a positive new outlook instead of dreading that you have to face another day.

"Thoughts produce feelings; Feelings produce emotion; Emotion is a powerful energy inside you that produces Motion; The more Motion you have, the more people you can help; The more people you help, the better life you lead; And it all comes down to the thoughts that occupy your mind."

— *Joseph J. Charbonneau*

Invest a few moments in that single greatest asset: You.

Let's work on an exercise that lays a strong foundation upon which you can build your new self-concept. Do you remember a few pages back when we discussed that picture you carry of yourself into the marketplace every day? We're going to start painting that picture and crystallizing your self-image.

But instead of using brushes and colors, we're going to use words. Here is a challenge for you to make a big step in taking control of your own life: Write down who you are as a human being. Write your identity.

Doing this one written exercise immediately places you in the top 3 percent of people in our society.

The spirit of Joe Charbonneau continually stands beside me and reminds me that my most important list is not *Today I'm Going to Do*. My very top list is titled, *"Today I'm Going to Be."* Every morning, I write down a short version of who I am that day, *then* the things that person needs to do.

We easily allow ourselves to get caught up in myriad little activities on a To-Do list, and we believe this makes us productive. It doesn't. It makes us busy. And busy-ness takes up our time and energy, and often keeps us from the Big Things that are truly important to us.

What makes us strong, what makes us productive, and what makes us know who we are so we know why we do what we do is the "To Be" part of the list at the top. And like other things in this book, I'm not telling you this is easy. It isn't.

That's why you're thinking about putting it off right now. That's why you're thinking thoughts like, "He might be onto something here. I'll get around to trying that later."

Noooooooooooo! Do it. Do it now. Do it right now.

In *Rocky III* when Apollo Creed and Rocky train on the beach after Rocky loses his inner confidence, Apollo screams at Rocky, "There *is* no tomorrow! There *is* no tomorrow!"

I'm really hammering on you to do this. It's the most important thing you can do to increase the value of your single greatest asset and take a huge step toward improving your life.

Choose to write your identity. You owe it to yourself. When was the last time you took time just to consider *you*? Step back and give yourself some room to think, to consider yourself. When you get to know you, it's kind of fun!

It was no short route to get where you are today. How did you get there? Who are you? Where did you come from? What are your most positive qualities? What would you like to improve? Like Joe Charbonneau asked me the very first time I met him, "What have you won at?"

This is a written exercise about you, by you, for you, and only you. It's your manifestation in black and white of who you really are, in your own terms.

This is critical to the mental and emotional health of successful salespeople because the stronger your sense of self in your inner core, the better you sell and the better you can deal with the consequences of our profession when they aren't in your favor.

Only Write Positive Affirmations

If you write down how you want to improve, make sure they are positive statements. No garbage. No negative thoughts allowed. If you want to stop overdrawing your checking account, don't make that your missive. Instead try something like, "I'm improving my finances and checkbook keeping skills."

Go ahead. Write your identity on the lines provided. Do it. Do it now. Do it right now. I'll wait.

After you finish your first draft, if you choose to build a stronger, deeper case for yourself about yourself, I highly recommend taking the Myers-Briggs Test.

The Myers-Briggs Test helps you understand your greatest asset.

An excellent self-analysis tool is available to you online: http://www.16personalities.com/

It's free, and it can be a great help when you write your identity.

"The Myers-Briggs Test is a scientifically validated assessment that measures your preferences on the four personality types created by Myers and Briggs," according to the website. But it goes far beyond the commonly referred to "four polar personality types" and refines your personal assessment among **16** different, very specific personalities.

For example, according to Myers-Briggs, your humble author is an **ENTP** ("The Debater"), who possesses Extroversion, Intuition, Thinking, Perception and is commonly summarized as someone who loves one exciting challenge after another. This is how the website, *16personalities.com,* describes it:

> "The ENTP personality type is the ultimate devil's advocate, thriving on the process of shredding arguments and beliefs and letting the ribbons drift in the wind for all to see. Unlike their more determined Judging (J) counterparts, ENTPs don't do this because they are trying to achieve some deeper purpose or strategic goal, but for the simple reason that it's fun. No one loves the process of mental sparring more than ENTPs, as it gives them a chance to exercise their effortlessly quick wit, broad accumulated knowledge base, and capacity for connecting disparate ideas to prove their points.
>
> "Taking a certain pleasure in being the underdog, ENTPs enjoy the mental exercise found in questioning the prevailing mode of thought, making them irreplaceable in reworking existing systems or shaking things up and pushing them in clever new directions.
>
> "However, they'll be miserable managing the day-to-day mechanics of actually implementing their suggestions. ENTP personalities love to brainstorm and think

> big, but they will avoid getting caught doing the 'grunt work' at all costs. ENTPs only make up about 3 percent of the population, which is just right, as it lets them create original ideas, then step back to let more numerous and fastidious personalities, handle the logistics of implementation and maintenance."

I don't include this so I can bare my soul on the world's laundry lines. I include it to illustrate the accuracy and depth this free online exercise provides for you. From the reading you've done up to this point, you may agree, *C'est moi,* guilty as charged. Now you see how I'm the argumentative, iconoclastic, cavalier product of an upbringing that was shaped by my father's "black-and-white" approach and my mother's "situational logic."

The Myers-Briggs exercise helps you pinpoint your current location in life, which helps you understand the contributing factors. It can help you understand yourself and how you relate to others. Believe me, this is one of those self-assessment processes that truly works.

I highly suggest you make time to go through this exercise. You have the motive (you're reading this book to help improve your understanding of yourself and your life), the means (just go to the website online), and the opportunity (it's FREE!). Don't shortchange yourself by putting it off until you forget about it.

"Follow the path of the unsafe, independent thinker. Expose your ideas to the dangers of controversy. Speak your mind and fear less the label of "crackpot" than the stigma of conformity. And on issues that seem important to you, stand up and be counted at any cost."

— Thomas J. Watson

"It's a real mother for ya..."

— Johnny "Guitar" Watson

Write Your Identity

I am ____________________________________

So What?

One of the great songs on the Hired Gun Play List is Billy Ocean's "When the Going Gets Tough, the Tough Get Going." It's time to get going. Write your identity. Rewrite your identity. Then, write it again. In a June 2011 interview with *Story in Literary Fiction,* Paul Engle, director of the Iowa Writer's Workshop, is quoted as saying, "Writing is rewriting what you've already rewritten."

Choose to write the single most important essay you may ever write. It doesn't have to be long. It can be one paragraph. You owe it to yourself to get it right. Review it daily. Rewrite it often as a work in constant progress. Determine what thoughts you want to change in your mind, and determine how to replace them. Then, do it.

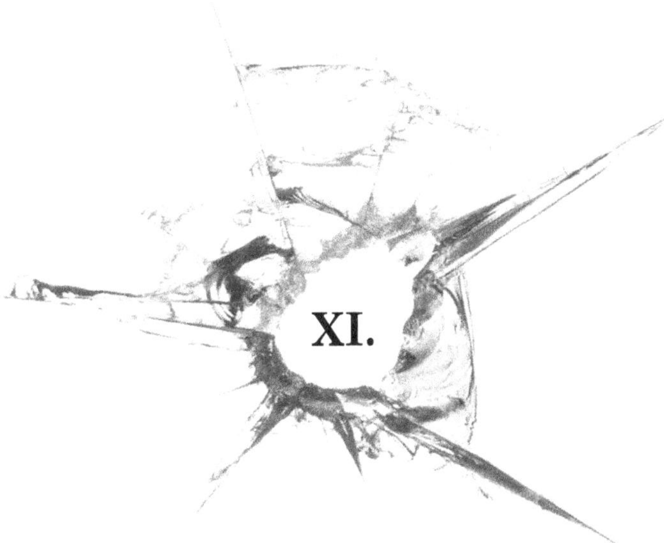

XI.

Your Single Greatest Power

In which your greatest asset becomes a foundation and fulcrum for leveraging your greatest power

When you master control over your single greatest asset, it establishes an unshakable fulcrum you can use to leverage your single greatest power. Another great book on the Hired Gun Suggested Reading List is *Your Greatest Power* by J. Martin Kohe. Spoiler Alert: He concludes that our greatest power is the power of choice. The book is timeless and inexpensive, and I highly recommend it. Here's a synopsis from Goodreads.com:

> "J. Martin Kohe shows you how to use your greatest power.... Many people can't be successful in the best of times because they have failed to make use of this greatest power...the power to choose. Other people will apply this greatest power...and be successful even in bad times because they refuse to let adversity stop them... they will persist until they succeed."

Think about it: When you boil things down to their simplest elements, life is comprised of an incredibly complex set of binary decisions called choices. Not unlike old mainframe computer cards, everything we do boils down to a 0 or a 1; it's a little box that's either filled in or left empty.

Do you wake up or continue to sleep? Do you have breakfast? One egg? Two eggs? Three? Do you floss today? Which shirt—not that one, not that one, not that one, but yes, that one. And so on, from turning right or left in your car, braking or not braking, accelerating or not to deciding between coffee, cream, and sugar at work.

Here's what you can choose that morning: Sleep in late, shirk breakfast because you just don't feel like making it, wear dumpy frumpy clothes you only put on to work in the yard where nobody sees you, leave the car in the garage because there isn't enough gas to drive to work, or call in sick. Hmmmm, probably not good choices.

Conversely, you can choose: Your best #1 power suit, your best #1 power shoes, wake up early to have plenty of time, and not feel rushed or stressed. You choose to make a big breakfast so you'll have energy through the day. Your car is in tiptop shape, clean, and full of gas so you can just go!

I caution you not to get hung up analyzing minutia and details of your everyday choices like those simple decisions. It can drive you crazy. The simple fact is, we all constantly exert this tremendous power to a greater or lesser extent as part of our inherent nature.

It's important to simply accept the fact that we all make many decisions all day long, and our actions are results of these decisions. All day, every day, we choose, and those choices are based upon things we've learned.

When we're faced with making a Big Decision, these smaller choices form a foundation upon which we build more choices to help us arrive at a pinnacle decision where we finally pull the trigger on The Big One.

Our decision pyramids are like works of art that are one big picture made up of a thousand smaller images or pointillist dots. These are marvels of human engineering. Somehow the color and content of each little picture tile fits into the overall image like a piece in a jigsaw puzzle, and when it's complete, we stand back and see the Big Picture.

It's the choices we make that lead to the circumstances of our lives.

— Law of the Hired Gun

There is always choice. We just have to be prepared to deal with the *consequences* of our choices and try in each instance to make the best choice we can with what we have at our disposal. We all sit around the table of life as cards are dealt to us. How you play your hand is up to you.

1/2 Point

This is just a small example, but at one company, our Junior Sales Suit figured out a novel way to bonus the sales team. He devised a convoluted schedule of factors involved in the deals we sold and determined a point value for each one. When we achieved a certain number of points, we received a paycheck bonus.

One month, I racked up some pretty good sales and was just 1/2 point away from a bonus worth several thousand dollars. I was totally focused on closing the deals at hand all month, and when I was conversationally reminded about "the points bonus," I only had a half day before the month ended to figure out a way to cash in. I was tired, and my pals were all going to lunch to celebrate their good fortunes. I wanted to finish up the month, relax, and enjoy an extended lunch break with the good company of my colleagues.

But I made a different choice and executed that decision. In a quiet, sequestered place, I pored over the list of convoluted PROCESSES and rules to achieve this bonus income. After I reviewed all the options available in this new plan, I figured out that I could get exactly 1/2 point if I got one of my new clients that month to move to a two-year contract instead of the standard one-year term.

I reviewed all my sales that month and found the one most likely to respond favorably if I approached him correctly. On my phone call to him, I pitched the potential benefits of locking in his reduced promotional subscription rate for an additional year and—BOOM!—$5,000 came into my hands.

That day, I had a lot of choices available to me. I could have decided that it wasn't worth the extra effort. But I chose not to go to lunch with my colleagues and celebrate the last day of the month as usual. I chose not to rest on the fact I had a good month and was ready for it to be over. There was still some distance left in the race I was running.

Instead, I compared the short-term gratification of strolling across the finish line and relaxing with my buddies versus the benefits of conquering this latest management game in the final hours. It was a conscious choice that resulted in solving a puzzle that significantly increased my income that month. I got the job done.

In the previous chapter, we examined the notion that thoughts produce feelings, feelings produce emotions, emotion is an energy that produces Motion, and the more Motion you have, the more people you can help. Drilling down just a bit deeper, I add this:

Thoughts produce feelings; Feelings produce emotions; Emotion is a powerful energy inside you that produces Motion; The more Motion you have the more people you can help; The more people you help the more money you can make; The more money you make the more choice you can have; The more choice you have, the better life you can lead.

— Law of the Hired Gun

Money Money Money Money...

Money is a tool that affords us choice. With more money, you have more choice. It's that plain and simple.

For example, let's say you want to buy a car and have $1,000. Your choices are pretty limited. On the other hand, let's say you have $100,000 available to buy your car. You have many, many more choices.

And that pretty much sums up the value of money.

The more money you have, the more capacity you have to make choices about your home, your car, your clothes, your food, your health insurance, your kids' school, clothes, and sports activities; the list is endless. And it all comes back to the thoughts that occupy your mind.

Your money is similar to a car's gas gauge, an indicator of how much choice you have in life. It isn't the amount of horsepower you have or your ability to stay in control while making quick changes in direction. Based on your values and standards, if your money gauge is full, you have a lot of choice. If it's near *E*, not so much.

If you want to have more money, if you want to learn how to improve your life, go directly to the source, and change the thoughts that occupy your mind.

How Do We Improve Our Thoughts?

There are generally two ways to predictably modify human behavior:

1) **Spaced repetition** over an extended period of time. This is the process used in school to teach most of us pretty much everything. You repeat an action spaced out over a period of time until the new behavior becomes automatic to you, like tying your shoe. A place kicker kicks thousands of footballs through goalposts. A pitcher throws thousands of pitches. We learn the multiplication tables over and over until we have them memorized.

2) **A significant emotional event.** This results in a quantum leap in the modification of human behavior. It short circuits typical spaced repetition learning by replacing that process with a single, high-impact incident. This event is so shocking and so strong that it alone causes immediate behavior change.

To differentiate between the two, spaced repetition provides predictable, desirable behavior change over an extended period of time. A significant emotional event can cause prodigious changes in behavior in an instant. But it really cannot be planned for; it happens, we react and respond. We learn.

For a simple example of a significant emotional event, the "wire hangers" scene in the movie *Mommie Dearest* comes to mind. Do you think that little girl ever uses wire hangers again after that single incident with her mother, Joan Crawford?

We can't do much to control the significant emotional events that take place in our lives, except to recognize them and pay attention to the way in which they affect our thoughts about ourselves and our future actions. But with spaced repetition, we can totally control which new thoughts enter our minds.

Sources for Self-Improvement

Where do we go to exercise our greatest power of choice and gather information that improves our thinking and changes our lives? Where can we find the positive rocks to displace the negative water in our minds? Where do we go to learn how to be a Master at anything?

The library. Yes. Go ahead, make a trip to your local library. It's an incredible place. It contains the written and recorded works of people through the ages who have mastered success in their chosen fields and want to tell you all about how to do it. Successful people love to share the principles and discoveries that helped them get where they are. These are the works of the Masters, and they're all available to you free, either onsite or to take home.

It doesn't cost much to use a library. A few dollars (if even that) for a library card, and you can usually keep your borrowed books for weeks. If you return a book late, there's a whopping fee of about 20 cents per day or less. You are limited to how many items you can check out at one time, sometimes up to 50!

It's cheap to learn how to improve your life. When you go to your library, here's what you'll see: An empty parking lot. Go inside, there's a lot of room to move around, find things to read and listen to, because there's often nobody there.

But go to a movie theatre! You can see all kinds of movies that have huge production budgets and impact our brains with CGI enhanced visual scenes, stirring dialogues, incredible special effects and music that show us the effects of alcohol, drugs, murder, rape, terrorism, theft, and war. Long lines, high ticket costs, and expensive concessions.

It costs a lot of money to learn how to screw up your life. But where you learn how to improve your life, it's free and empty.

Consider this: James Cameron, the famous director of movies like *Terminator, Terminator 2, The Abyss, Titanic,* and *Avatar,* worked at odd jobs and was driving a truck when he decided to go to the USC library. There, he read everything he could find about filmmaking written by graduate students in the USC film school. Several blockbuster movies and two Academy Awards later for Best Director, and the rest is history.

The Internet is another place to find good information. It's also a place where you can find all manner of things better left alone. Once again, it's your choice. You can find books, movies, and just about everything you want to see or learn about online with ease. It's the most ingenious research device ever invented. If you don't have a computer, you can usually use or rent time on one at your local library.

Seminars in self-improvement are all around us. Some are great, and some are well, less than great. It all depends on the quality of the presenter. There are a lot of big names I wouldn't pay 50 cents to see, and there are a lot of people with great messages that don't charge nearly enough.

Make the time; go to them. You will learn quickly how to judge for yourself the people and subjects that strike home to you. Especially check out the free presentations. Of course, they're free so that they can convince you to pay to go to bigger, longer, more in-depth seminars or workshops held later in your community, and you may or may not elect to sign up for their bigger sessions. But I've learned that in every instance, even those where the presentation is crummy or the content is spurious, you always come away learning at least one valuable new piece of information.

Motivation? Information?

There are largely two kinds of self-improvement seminars: Motivation or Information.

Motivational Seminars: I'm sure you've been to these or seen them advertised on billboards across your highways. Motivational Rallies feature a number of very high profile, highly paid speakers and they all do a great job. They tell us and show us how wonderful we are (right!), that we can achieve great things (right again!), that our destinies are under our own control, and we can Dare to Be Great! (right, yet again!).

Here's the problem with motivational seminars: These massive presentations to mass audiences at huge event centers also inadvertently hurt a lot of people. The missions of motivational seminars are altruistic, the speakers are powerful, and their messages generate a lot of excitement and energy. Many people leave the event and feel imbued to make changes in their lives.

The problem is that 48 hours after the rally ends, it's human nature that we tend to forget 50 percent of what we heard. Three weeks later, we've forgotten 80 percent of what we heard. It's a natural limitation of human memory. In the meantime, people make choices and decisions about their lives based on what they heard or remember they heard.

But there is no information about How to Do It. We're told we can be great but nobody shows us how to be great or how to improve ourselves. There isn't time for actual lessons. There are too many highly paid speakers. People go out and try something new, inspired and motivated by new passions, perhaps even to try something they've feared.

Unfortunately, they don't know *how* to do it and fail. Then they see this all as just one more time they tried to improve and failed, and they lapse into depression.

The result of a lot of motivational seminars and rallies is they produce a bunch of excited failures; in other words, they produce a lot of passionate people running around without the knowledge and information they need to take advantage and leverage that newfound enthusiasm. That's why I'm not really a big fan of motivational seminars and rallies, and ask not to be billed as a "motivational speaker" when I speak.

Information Seminars: Informational seminars or workshops provide just the opposite. There isn't a lot of motivational talk because this is a presentation of information about a subject. This is where we truly learn how to do something new that benefits us.

But again, these gatherings suffer from our human limitations. We still forget 50 percent of what we heard after 48 hours, and we still forget 80 percent of what we heard three weeks later. The good news is, with good notes or recordings (if allowed), we can recoup the information later.

The problem is, if we're not motivated to use this new information, it's still not much use to us. The result is that there are often a lot of intellectual mediocre people produced by informational seminars because they don't possess the confidence, commitment, desire, determination, and energy to put those new ideas into effect. So once again, people fail after attending. They've learned some great new ideas but don't have the self-image or motivation to put them into effect in their lives.

Think about it this way: If someone has a self-image of five on a scale of 0-10, and they're provided with new skills information with a value of 10, do you think that they can see themselves operating at a higher level with this new information? During a 44-city tour, Joe and I learned from hundreds of personal interviews with salespeople that a person cannot possibly see themselves operating at a level of 10 if they see themselves operating only at a level of five and put only 50 percent of who they are into what they do. As Joe used to tell me, "I've never seen a poor person who could teach anyone how to get rich."

That would be like thinking that a junior varsity football player can watch a football game and visualize and understand the refined skills of an NFL veteran professional. Or it's like sales reps who just want to work for their paychecks and go home. They think, "At least I showed up." They don't expect much back because they don't put much in.

If they only believe in themselves 50 percent, or rate themselves as fives on a scale of 0-10, that's as much as they have to give: 50 percent. When this is the case, they can only use half their value and cannot possibly envision what it's like for a nine or a 10 to benefit from something.

I'm not knocking all of these motivational and informational events. But I am knocking those that hurt people by providing half of what we need in order to truly improve our lives.

Motivational and informational seminars can be extremely helpful; they can also be damaging. You want to be sure you understand what you're going to see so you have a much better idea of what you can expect to get out of it and set realistic expectations. Again, exercise your single greatest power of choice when attending a self-help seminar or workshop.

Classes are available to you through local schools, community colleges, churches, and other local organizations. Plus, there are often local groups that host informal classes for people who really just want to learn.

So What?

The options and opportunities exist; they're out there. We just need to find them, choose one that might be a good place to begin, and—do it—make the time to go.

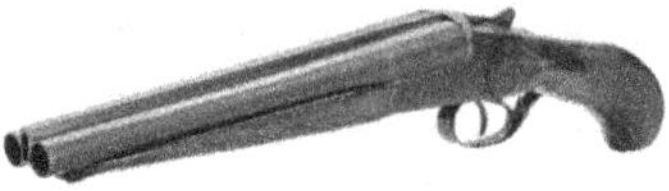

XII.

Sales Provides the Best Return on Investment (ROI) of Any Career

In which we compare the Return on Investment of a career in sales versus the top licensed professions of doctors, lawyers, and architects

During my darkest years of adolescence, I was a confused mass of indecision. Which college do I want to attend? What will be my major? What do I want to study? What do I want to do with my life? Pretty much the same as any other high school junior or senior.

One day, I experienced an epiphany and asked my dad if we could talk about it.

He asked, "What is it you want to talk about?"

I was ready to impress him. I said, "I've given a lot of thought to what I want to be in life and I've finally figured it out." I even paused for dramatic effect. "I want to be a doctor," I said. Because he was a doctor, I expected to see him smile. I expected maybe a little button to burst off his chest with pride. I thought I was prepared for just about anything.

But I didn't plan on the immediate belly laugh I received in reply.

Dumbfounded, I paused, then asked, "What do you mean?"

He was still laughing. "Oh, I hated that job."

I never thought of having a medical practice as a job. It seemed more like a calling with the Hippocratic Oath, all that kind of stuff. The guy who was laughing at that notion was my dad, my mentor. Along with my mother, he was my intellectual and social standard-bearer for excellence.

My personal field of vision was narrow and myopic. I was old enough to appreciate my father's work only in the later years of his career, decades after he had left his private practice. All my life I had seen him as a medical officer in the US Navy, atop the world's scientific community as he spearheaded revolutionary advances in decompression medicine, and supervised divers' work undersea at depths of more than 1,000 feet.

I somehow mentally misplaced my mother's stories about his private general practice in rural Iowa. When he was a young family practitioner, he carried a snow shovel in the trunk of his car so when he made winter house calls out on farms, he could shovel the snow a few feet, advance his car, shovel a few more, advance again, and repeat the process until he got to his call.

Fishing is a huge sport in rural Iowa, and his practice consisted of numerous fish hook removals from all parts of the body. One time, he had to remove a fishing lure from a woman's eye.

When we took my cat to the vet for its annual shots, the shots cost something like three dollars each. When we got back home, my dad remarked, "That's more than I used to charge for shots to my patients."

So much for my career in medicine.

Gidget Goes to College

First, let's look at the costs of a typical college undergraduate degree program.

CollegeBoard.org is a website dedicated to helping high school and prep students work through the process of testing, applying, and choosing a college. They post a chart on their site to help aspiring collegians plan ahead with *Average Estimated Undergraduate Budgets, 2017-2018.*

Their chart shows all related costs: Tuition and Fees, Room and Board, Books and Supplies, Transportation, and Other Expenses. Here is a summary of their findings for average annual costs at various institutions of higher learning:

Public Two-Year, In-District, Commuter - $17,580
Public Four-Year, In-State, On-Campus - $25,290
Public Four-Year, Out of State, On-Campus - $40,940
Private Non-Profit, Four Year, On-Campus - $50,900

It can cost anywhere from $35,000 for a two-year degree, commuting locally, to more than $200,000 for a four-year degree from a private school. And this simply sets the stage for the top licensed professions: doctors, lawyers, and architects, all noble and highly respected callings.

Let's see how these numbers stack up against a career in sales.

Physicians

Let's begin by looking at doctors. How many years in college? Four years of undergraduate study, followed by four intense competitive years of medical school, one year of internship, then there are two to seven more years of residency depending upon which kind of specialty skills might be pursued. For psychiatry, add another four years of school.

According to the Association of American Medical Colleges, the recent average annual tuition rate at a public US medical school is $34,592 for in-state students and $58,668 if they attend from out of state.

Private medical schools average more than $50,000 a year, regardless whether you're an in-state or out-of-state student. These tuition rates do not include books, computers, room and board, and other personal costs. This can all add up quickly to a six-figure student debt.

Let's say the doctor in question eventually opens a new practice. What are the costs involved? Business start-up fees, malpractice insurance. (In Florida, malpractice insurance can easily range from $50,000 to $70,000 per year.) For OB/GYNs, malpractice insurance can be as high as $200,000 per year.

Then there are lease fees for a small startup office space of about 1,500 square feet. For office renovations and improvements, add another $20,000 to $50,000. Add some office equipment like computers, file cabinets, office furniture, printers/copiers, waiting room furnishings, and amenities, and you can add another $100,000 to the tab.

But that's just getting ready to get ready.

Then there are active continuing costs of advertising, domain name, website creation and monitoring, business cards, stationery, medical practice consultant fees, tax and legal advisors, office rent and utilities, medical equipment and materials, (x-ray machine?), property insurance, payroll for office staff ranging from $35,000 to $65,000 per year for each person, business taxes, self-employment tax, and professional development.

Kathy Kristof, in an article for *CBS MoneyWatch* headlined, "$1 Million Mistake: Becoming a Doctor," writes,

> If you are brilliant, ambitious, and gifted in science, you may consider becoming a doctor. If so, think twice. According to a new survey by personal finance site NerdWallet, most doctors are dissatisfied with the job, and less than half would choose a career in medicine if they were able to do it all over again.

A May 2018 article by Pauline Anderson on Medscape, "Physicians Experience Highest Suicide Rate of Any Profession," raises another issue: suicide.

> "With one completed suicide every day, US physicians have the highest suicide rate of any profession," she writes. "In addition, the number of physician suicides is more than twice that of the general population, new research shows."

But There is Good News!

On Aug. 16, 2018, New York University Medical School announced that it would provide free tuition to current and future medical students. According to an article in Modern Healthcare, "NYU leaders called the decision a 'moral imperative' considering the impact medical school debt has on physician stress levels, diversity in the profession and the provider shortage.'" NYU is raising funds through endowments and has been building a war chest to pay for the initiative for the past 11 years.

<u>Projected income for physicians</u>:
According to the Bureau of Labor and Statistics for 2016: $196,380 average annual income.

Attorneys

The minimum investment in education and time for a JD law degree is four years of undergraduate study, followed by three years of law school. For a master's degree, add one more year, and for a Doctor of Judicial Science, add three more.

On April 6, 2017, *U.S. News and World Report* reported that the average cost of tuition and fees at private law schools for the 2016-2017 academic year was about $43,000, while the average in-state and out-of-state cost of tuition and fees at public schools was about $26,000 and $39,000. The top 10 law schools averaged over $40,000 per year for tuition alone.

U.S. News also published a list of 181 US law schools, asking, "Which law school graduates have the most debt?" It shows the average amount of post-graduate student debt, plus the percent of graduates with debt. I added up all 181 schools and divided to obtain the average, about $118,000 of student debt per student per law school. I performed the same addition and division to determine the average percent of law school graduates who leave school with debt: about 80 percent.

Ilana Kowarski's article, "See the Price, Payoff of Law School Before Enrolling" in *U.S. News and World Report* online in March 2018, reported, "The median private sector salary among 2016 graduates from the 180 ranked law schools that provided these data to *U.S. News* in an annual survey was $68,375."

Projected income: According to the Bureau of Labor and Statistics for 2016: $118,160 average annual income.

And then there's suicide. In a June 2018 *Connecticut Law Review* article, "Alarming Increase in Suicide Rate Needs to be Addressed Everywhere," Mark Dubois writes,

> "A 2016 report of the ABA (American Bar Association) and Hazelden Institute revealed 19 percent of lawyers responding reporting mild or higher levels of anxiety, 20.6 percent with problem drinking, 28 percent with mild or worse depression and 11.5 percent reporting suicidal thoughts. The Dave Nee Foundation reports that lawyers are the most frequently depressed occupational group in the US, lawyers are 3.6 times more likely to suffer from depression than nonlawyers, depression and anxiety is cited by 26 percent of all lawyers who seek counseling, 15 percent of people with clinical depression commit suicide and lawyers rank fifth in incidence of suicide by occupation."

Architects

The typical college undergraduate program for a Bachelor's in Architecture is five years. For a snapshot overview of becoming licensed in this profession, check out this information from the website DataUSA:

Total degrees awarded in 2016: 10,000
Median in-state public tuition: $8,200
Median out-of-state private tuition: $45,000
Average salary: $77,000

The research team at DesignIntelligence, a firm dedicated to "Trends, Strategies, Research for Architect and Design Professionals," performed its own survey of 2,654 hiring professionals in the field of architecture to rank the top US architecture schools. Below is a list of DesignIntelligence's 2017-2018 top-rated US architecture schools and their relative costs of tuition:

1) The California Polytechnic State University at San Luis Obispo: $22,000/year in-state; $33,000/year out-of-state
2) Cornell University in New York: $60,000/year
3) Rice University: $53,000
4) The University of Texas at Austin: $22,000/year in-state; $46,000/year out-of-state
5) Virginia Polytechnic Institute and State University: $21,000 in-state; $36,000 out of state

Architect Graduate School

If you want to obtain a graduate degree in architecture, the annual tuition rates are even higher. Consider:

1) Harvard University Graduate School of Design: $65,000/year
2) Yale University: $64,000
3) Columbia University in New York City: $49,000/year
4) M.I.T. (nine months): $43,000
5) Cornell University: $47,000
5) Rice University: $29,000

The average out-of-state tuition at these top five architecture graduate schools computes to $55,220/year. Again, for architecture schools in general, median out-of-state tuition at a public school is $45,000/year.

What's the return on this investment? The US Department of Labor Statistics released this information in March 2018:

US architects earn between $47,480 and $134,610 a year.

Half of all architects (median income) earned $78,470 ($37.72 per hour).

Landscape architects make a bit less, from $38,950 and $106,770.

When I was in college, an upperclassman friend I admired went through the university's outstanding five-year architecture school and got his degree. Later, I ran into him when I walked into a barber shop and saw that he was sweeping up hair off the floor to make ends meet while he essentially apprenticed at a firm. Five years of calculus, trigonometry, physics, stress factors of building materials, art classes, and drawing classes = sweeping up hair.

In the first week of June 2016, the Centers for Disease Control and Prevention published a new report that compared professionals in architecture and engineering to other jobs and stated they are the fifth most likely group to commit suicide.

Do I admire doctors, lawyers, and architects, and many other licensed professions for what they do? Without doubt.

Do I think they got a good Return on Investment? No.

Sales

Sales offers the best ROI of any job or career, by far.

What are your start-up costs? Zero.

What are your educational requirements? None.

What is your income potential? Unlimited!

Unlimited? Yes! In sales, you truly do have the opportunity to make as much as you can, as fast as you can, as long as you can. *U.S. News and World Report Best Jobs Rankings* reported in 2016 these US Bureau of Labor Statistics numbers for sales "salaries":

25th percentile: $39,000
Median income: $57,140
75th percentile: $82,000
Top 10 percent of salespeople: $121,000

To be clear, I'm a big fan of *U.S. News*. Their journalistic quality and integrity have been above reproach for decades. And I have every confidence that their numbers in this report are accurate, as they are in the other reports. I'm also sure the sales profession provides a very nice standard of living for reps who earn income levels shown on this list.

But I wish this report illustrated just a little better the upside income figures for sales. I also really wish the entire report wasn't based on "salary."

How many sales reps do you know that are paid a "salary?"

I'm going to let that one twist in the wind for a moment.

The title of this *U.S. News* report is, "Sales Representative *Salary*." The very first line reads, "The median annual *salary* for a sales representative was $57,140 in 2016, according to the BLS." This would be all right if the figure above represented the median salary *base* or the amount of *draw against commission*. Unfortunately, "salary" is incorrectly used as a term synonymous with "total compensation."

This is like reading a report on the relative performance measurements of javelin throwers as if they were shot put measurements or on the fastball speed ratings of major league pitchers as if they were throwing footballs.

The use of the term "Sales Representative *Salary*" is an oxymoron. It's inaccurate, and the idea of salaried salespeople sends a shiver up my spine. It gives the feeling of being gently nudged into a box of conformity by the "everyone else does it that way" sheep mentality, a mentality I cannot help but resist.

I'm a sales professional, and sales professionals are not compensated with *salaries*. That's the reason most of us go into sales. Sales is not a punch-the-time-clock job compensated by a *salary*. It's a job compensated by *opportunity*.

Merriam-Webster online defines "salary" simply as, "fixed compensation paid regularly for services." The operative term here is "fixed compensation." So, you sell $1 million of revenue one month but only $10,000 the next, and you're paid the same amount each month "regularly for services."

There goes Aretha Franklin singing again: "Who's Zoomin' Who?"

Sales in Name Only

Other than the occasional car dealership that wants to advertise that its sales staff is not compensated based on commissions, I don't know of any other sales positions that are reimbursed based on a "fixed compensation paid regularly for services." If there are any, they're Sales in Name Only or SINOs.

But let's take a quick moment to examine even that one sales environment: A car dealership that features a noncommissioned sales staff. To do that, there is probably no better place to look than Edmunds, Inc./Edmunds.com. Since 1966, Edmunds has published new and used automotive pricing guides to help consumers and is a respected authority in the area of auto sales.

In 2014, Senior Editor Matt Jones, who writes for Edmunds with a 12-year track record as a car salesman, internet sales manager, and finance and insurance manager, wrote the article, "*Saying Goodbye to Commission Based Car Salespeople.*" In it, he says the following:

> 1) Topic sentence: "A growing number of car dealerships have moved away from paying their salespeople profit-based commission."
> 2) Historical reference: "Traditional sales commissions are calculated as a percentage of the profit from a sale. The more money a car dealership makes on the sale, the more the salesperson earns."
> 3) Reality versus Ideology: "But the cost of hiring and training salespeople has run smack into another issue: profit on new cars and trucks has been in decline...according to the National Automobile Dealers Association (NADA)."
> 4) Concluding paragraph: "With lower profit margins on new car sales come smaller commissions. Salespeople often earn just a 'mini'—industry slang for minimum commission—of $50 to $150 on each car sold. Given that the average salesperson sells 10 cars per month, that adds up to a meager income. **If minis are all they're making, a commissioned salesperson may decide the grass is greener elsewhere.**"

Apparently, the problem with noncommissioned sales is there's not enough compensation to retain true top-level talent. Previously, salespeople were compensated on a percentage of the profit on a car sale, so profits were higher. But with this new compensation plan, profits are lower because there are no top-tier sales reps selling higher profit margins on the cars; the good sales reps can't make any money and have to move on, leaving behind the mediocre reps. The A-Team leaves, and the B-Team takes over.

Now you've got a mediocre dealership staffed with a bunch of mediocre sales reps who make mediocre pay. I don't know about you but a mediocre environment is not where a Hired Gun-quality sales rep is going to hang around.

LESSON FOR SALES MANAGERS:

The previous scenario shows how medium expectations yield low results.

If you want to run a team of mediocre salespeople, pay them "salaries."

High expectations = High results
Medium expectations = Low results
Low expectations = No results

— **Law of the Hired Gun**

Salespeople Are Not Salaried Employees

Some people argue that salespeople should be compensated the same way that everyone else in a company is paid, on a salary. Well, you just saw what is happening in cases where it's being tried. End result = mediocrity. Show me the CEO who wants to report that to the company's shareholders.

I didn't spend 40 years in sales to be mediocre. I didn't spend four decades in sales to punch a clock. I didn't bust my ass 10-12 hours every day, plus weekends, to earn a "salary." The sales department operates by different conventions than production, accounting, HR, and IT, and it's compensated differently.

Why? Below is an accurate summarization of sales compensation as reported under the subject heading "Commissions" on the US Department of Labor website:

> "A sales commission is a sum of money paid to an employee upon completion of a task, usually selling a certain amount of goods or services. Employers sometimes use sales commissions as incentives to increase worker productivity."

Again, the operative words here are: "...as incentives to increase worker productivity."

That's why salespeople don't punch timeclocks. That's why we work until 3:00 a.m. That's why we come in on weekends. That's why we resist like the plague any impediments that distract us from being able to "increase worker productivity."

It's difficult to measure normal office-bound jobs in a way that could put some kind of commissioned compensation plan into effect. It's never been done at anyplace I've ever worked, and I'm sure if it could be done, it would have been done by now. I've never seen it. Other departments can't really show clear black-and-white contributions to the company's bottom line on a spreadsheet, so it makes sense that they're paid based on a "fixed compensation paid regularly for services."

Top-tier sales reps may have a base draw against their commissions and/or a base pay rate as part of their overall compensation plan, but the bulk of a salesperson's *income* is earned by commissions as a percentage of revenue produced. A salesperson's take home pay is *income*, not a *salary*. The sound of the term "salary" has the effect, to me, of someone scraping their fingernails on a chalkboard.

To figure out why any business might consider trying to experiment with sales compensation like this, refer to the Primary Law of the Hired Gun: "Whenever in doubt, always look for the financial incentive."

The Suits figure it will cost the company less this way.

If the Suits are compensated by salaries that are not directly tied to the performance of the company and the revenue to the bottom line, why not? It's no skin off their noses if revenues drop. But I don't think The Boss will be crazy about it.

Back to the Salesperson's income chart: The 75th percentile makes about $82,000. I mean, even in today's economy, if you're making $82,000 life doesn't stink. But please understand, as we saw on the *U.S. News* chart, the numbers shown are all for the *bottom 90 percent* of this profession.

And this is another place I take exception to the findings of the report. It also states, "The best-paid 10 percent made roughly $121,080, while the lowest-paid earned approximately $27,500."

The—Best Paid—salespeople—the top 10 percent in the entire US of A made about $121,000? In 2016?

Come on, "Who's Zoomin' Who?" I made more than that in my *first* sales job at 29, 30, 31, 32, 33, 34 years of age in the '80s. Thirty-five years ago. Please, please, please understand this is again no brag, just fact. I just don't agree with the outcomes in this "Sales Representative *Salary*" report, and my own track record is the basis for my disagreement. I'm not challenging the data; I'm challenging the conclusions.

In Joe Charbonneau's *Forward* to the original *HIRED GUN,* he wrote, "During the next fast-paced years, I watched him [your humble author] grow to achieve an income and lifestyle enjoyed by only the top 2 percent."

That's the kind of sales rep I'm talking about. That's the Return on Investment—the ROI—I'm interested in.

"You Can Make Incredible Sums of Money in Enterprise Software Sales" is a September 2014 article posted on BusinessInsider.com by Julie Bort. At that time, according to the Bureau of Labor Statistics as referenced in the article, **the average salary across all jobs in the US was $46,000.** Ms. Bort, however, writes that,

> The top 10 percenters "make from high [in] the $200s to low [in]the $400s, and are cranking in that zone, year after year," McEwan says. [Paul McEwan, partner for technical sales recruiter, Richard, Wayne, and Roberts.]

> In a really good year, a top salesperson at these companies can even earn $1 million, says Eliot Burdett, CEO of headhunting firm Peak Sales Recruiting.
>
> But it's tricky for them. **Salespeople are paid a base salary plus commission,** and the commission structure can be complicated, Burdett says. An enterprise software salesperson will have a quota, perhaps $5 million.
>
> Hit the quota and it's "cha-ching!"
>
> Miss it and risk losing your job.
>
> Salespeople who regularly exceed their quota will find that the company raises it.
>
> They should get paid more, but they'll also have more pressure to perform.

Below are snapshots of some sales reps (names omitted) who perform at this level, as cited in the *Business Insider* article:

Washington: Highest ever income, $300,000 to $400,000
Outside Rep/Field Sales, Washington
Previous Employer(s): Oracle, BEA, IBM
Product Expertise: Enterprise Application Integration/B2B Integration, Internet Infrastructure Software, Business Intelligence, Database & File Management Software
Vertical Expertise: Health care & Medical, Industrial Manufacturing
Largest Deal Ever Closed: Greater than $2 million
Highest Ever W2: $300,000 to $400,000
Average W2 Last Four Years: $250,000 to $350,000

North Carolina: Highest ever income, $300,000 to $400,000
Outside Rep/Field Sales, North Carolina
Previous Employer(s): SAP, Siebel, Oracle
Product Expertise: Enterprise Resource Planning (ERP), Supply Chain Management (SCM), Vertical Specific Solutions, Business Intelligence, Customer Relationship Management
Vertical Expertise: Industrial Manufacturing, Capital Equipment, Consumer Goods

Largest Deal Ever Closed: Greater than $2 million
Highest Ever W2: $300,000 to $400,000
Average W2 Last Four Years: $250,000 to $350,000

New York: Highest ever income, $300,000 to $400,000
Outside Rep/Field Sales, New York
Previous Employer(s): TIBCO, Information Builders, Computer Associates
Product Expertise: Enterprise Application Integration/B2B Integration, Internet Infrastructure Software, Systems & Network Management, Business Intelligence
Vertical Expertise: Mid-Market, Pharmaceuticals & Biotechnology, Financial Services
Largest Deal Ever Closed: Greater than $2 million
Highest Ever W2: $300,000 to $400,000
Average W2 Last Four Years: $150,000 to $250,000

Southern California: Highest ever income, $400,000 to $500,000
Outside Rep/Field Sales, Southern California
Previous Employer(s): Oracle
Product Expertise: CAD/CAM Software, Business Intelligence
Vertical Expertise: Financial Services, Aerospace
Largest Deal Ever Closed: Greater than $2 million
Highest Ever W2: $400,000 to $500,000
Average W2 Last Four Years: $250,000 to $350,000

Where do you learn to be a top-tier sales rep?

Two types of people are reading this book: Top gun sales reps or someone who aspires to become one of those reps. If you're in the former group, you're reading this because you know that, "You're either green and growing or you're ripe and rotten." You're always looking for new information to help you grow. If you're in the latter group, here's briefly what it takes to become a Hired Gun:

- **Improve your level of self-concept, self-belief, self-image.**
- **Pay your dues.**
- **Get out there and get your nose bloodied.**
- **Learn from your colleagues.**
- **Choose a mentor.**
- **Invest in your single greatest asset — you — with education, sales equipment, tools, gadgets, and clothes.**
- **Go to the best available sources.**

For your convenience, below is a list of some of the top sales speakers and trainers in the world today, along with their websites. I highly recommend visiting them for more information about the outstanding sales training and sales culture improvement programs available:

Jeffrey Gitomer - www.Gitomer.com - The Sales King - Click the button on his homepage: "Here's How I Can Help You." Author of *The Little Red Book of Selling, The Little Black Book of Connections,* plus *Platinum, Gold, Green, Teal,* and many other books, webinars, podcasts, and online training. Right now, if there is one guy who can help you win sales immediately, he is it.

Brian Tracy - www.BrianTracy.com - Simply the Best. The global eminent speaker and trainer on all things business, sales, management, speaking, and personal development. Brian is the author of *Maximum Achievement* and *Advanced Selling Strategies,* published by Simon & Schuster and *The 100 Absolutely Unbreakable Laws of Business Success* published by Berrett Koehler.

Jim Cathcart - www.Cathcart.com - Jim Cathcart was chosen one of the "Top Sales Influencers of 2014, 2015 and 2016" by *Top*

Sales World Magazine based in London & Paris, and he is listed as a Top Sales Influencer. He was selected as the #9 "Top 25 Speaker" in 2017 out of 1,300 speakers in an online survey by Speaking.com. He is also the best-selling author of 19 books, including his latest, *The Will To Win.*

Thom Winninger - www.Winninger.com - "Discover your purpose and realize your full potential." This world-class speaker and sales trainer is unbelievably accessible. If you go to his website, you will see his open invitation: "Feel free to contact me! Whether you have a question, comment, request, thought or experience, feel free to reach out, and I will reach back!" My only question is, what are you waiting for?

Dr. Tony Alessandra - www.alessandra.com - I personally absolutely love and admire a person like Dr. Tony. His offerings are so vast and his experience so great, it's best to summarize directly from the homepage of his website: "Dr. Alessandra has a streetwise, college-smart perspective on business, having been raised in the housing projects of NYC to eventually realizing success as a graduate professor of marketing, internet entrepreneur, business author, and hall-of-fame keynote speaker. He earned a BBA from Notre Dame, an MBA from the University of Connecticut and his PhD in marketing in 1976 from Georgia State University." It goes on to say, "His focus is on how to create instant rapport with prospects, employees and vendors; how to convert prospects and customers into business apostles who will 'preach the gospel' about your company and products; and how to out-market, out-sell and out-service the competition."

I will put him in perspective this simple way: Your friendly neighborhood Hired Gun has written two business books. Dr. Tony has written 30. 'Nuff Said.

Dr. Nido R. Qubein - www.nidoqubein.com - "Dr. Nido Qubein came to the United States as a teenager with little knowledge of English, no contacts and only $50 in his pocket. His life has been an amazing success story.

As a professional speaker, Dr. Qubein has received many distinctions. Toastmasters International named him Top Business and Commerce Speaker and awarded him the Golden Gavel Medal. He is the youngest person ever inducted in the International Hall of Fame and is the founder of the prestigious National Speakers Foundation in Phoenix, Arizona. He is in great demand to speak to business and professional groups around the world each year. He has been the recipient of many honors, including the Ellis Island Medal of Honor, the Horatio Alger Award for Distinguished Americans, the Order of the Long Leaf Pine (North Carolina's highest civic award), a Doctorate of Law degree, Sales and Marketing International's Ambassador of Free Enterprise, Citizen of the Year, and Philanthropist of the Year in his home city of High Point, NC, induction into the Global Society for Outstanding Business Leadership, and dozens more.

Dr. Qubein also is the president of High Point University in North Carolina, chairman of Great Harvest Bread Company, and serves on the boards of directors for: BB&T Bank, La-Z-Boy, and DOT Furniture.

These magnificent sales and business leaders are all available to help you improve your game. They've helped me, and they are as close to you as their websites. As much as I hate to repeat myself, what are you waiting for?

Sure, many job postings for sales positions typically state something like, "BS degree required with three to five years of sales experience." This may be the case for a lot of sales jobs, but where do you get that three to five years of experience? Hint: You don't get it in a four-year institution that costs you $50,000 annually for tuition (plus about $15,000 per year for living expenses).

You get sales experience in sales jobs that pay you money. The sales profession is the king of On the Job training because These Things You Don't Learn in School.

There is no educational requirement for excellence, and there is none for sales. You don't have to spend four to 10 years in school.

Look, one friend of mine reached the pinnacle of the high-tech profession when she became the CIO for two different companies, both among the nation's top five homebuilders. She had a high school education. Another friend of mine is the CFO and vice president of finance for a major national media corporation. His accomplishments there are the envy of his peers. He doesn't have a CPA.

1) You can make money in sales right away with a fifth grade education.

2) There is no business start-up cost for sales.

3) The income potential is unlimited!

Even in the beginning, it isn't likely you'll sweep hair at a barbershop to make ends meet. Remember, I got my first job in sales because I was a writer. What are the odds of that?

I'm not at all knocking the value of a higher education; I'm the product of one. In sales, your major doesn't matter nor do your areas of interests; at the very *least*, the education you obtain at an institution of higher learning gives you a tremendously enhanced frame of reference for everything that goes on around you.

A good education helps you develop a studied process of thinking, creating, and solving problems. You learn how to write well, something that benefits you the rest of your life regardless of occupation. All of these learned processes are helpful in any job you take down the road. College work in any of the fields of communications, psychology, business, and marketing can be valuable in the career of a professional salesperson.

It often isn't about what you know but how you use it. For example, when I went through the graduate screenwriting sequence at the University of Texas, we were largely accepted into the program due to our work backgrounds or degrees held in radio, television, or film. But a friend of mine entered our graduate school TV production course with a major in history. Of course, several of us wondered how far she would go with such a limited broadcast media background. Just a few short years later, she became the executive producer of three major hit TV shows on ABC.

Your acquired wealth of knowledge when you leave an institution of higher learning always pays off. In sales, an entourage effect occurs. Your expanded thinking, your increased ability to process information, and your ability to write well are all collectively helpful in sales because our sales skills are augmented by our general life experiences, possibly more than any other profession.

The more you know about things, the better salesperson you can be, and the greater knowledge base you have to relate to unfamiliar people and businesses. Think about it this way: What prospective client wouldn't cursorily enjoy a sales call discussion with someone who majored in astronomy? (I finagled admission to Astronomy 808 for myself and my roommate, Homer Dean from Abilene. This was the most advanced undergraduate class in the astronomy department with about 10 course prerequisites in higher math and science that we had not taken. Needless to say, we were politely asked to leave.)

Or how about this: A college friend of mine spent a summer between semesters in Greece working as a shepherd. An honest to goodness, staff in hand, minder of sheep. In Greece. He always listed it on his resumes because it turned job interviews into friendly conversations and steered them away from the normal interview babble.

There really is no replacement for a higher education. It just isn't *required* when going into sales. With sales, you can get started with the most minimal of investments and can reap the highest income rewards. Plus, it prepares you to advance to starting your own business, which can't thrive without successful sales.

Supply and Demand

In July 2018, I performed a quick online job search for available sales job postings by job title. The most interesting online service posts job opportunities in Hollywood and is called "Deadline Jobs" (http://jobs.deadline.jobs.com). Why did I choose to look there? Because I wanted to take a quantitative look for sales jobs available in industries we might not normally think of for sales job postings.

I wanted to stack the deck against sales and see how the profession stacks up in industries known for just about anything, except sales. It turns out, the entertainment industry is clamoring for sales reps!

When you think of the entertainment industry, what jobs do you think of? Actors and actresses? Singers? Wrestlers? Producers, writers, directors, editors, and camera operators but probably not sales.

Below is a brief quantitative comparison of how many job postings Deadline Jobs showed on one day, listed in order of the available quantity of postings by job title:

Producer: 31
Account Executive: 27
Reporter: 26
Other: 18
Photographer: 12
Editor: 9
Executive Producer: 8
News Producer: 6
Production Technician: 6
Assignment Editor: 6
Internship: 6
Production Assistant: 5
Studio Technician: 5
Photojournalist: 4
Physical Therapist: 4
Assistant Sales: 4
Sales Coordinator: 3
International Sales Manager: 3
Graphic Artist: 3
Promotions: 3
Graphic Designer: 3
Associate Producer: 2
Engineer: 2
Entertainer: 2
Faculty: 2
Associate Producer: 2
Creative Director: 2
Line Producer: 2
News Writer: 2
Quality Control Technician: 2
Traffic Coordinator: 2
Web Producer: 2
Writer: 2
...and a whole bunch of job titles with just one listing...

Of course, the euphi-title used for sales here is "account executive." But in their Hollywood entertainment industry job listings, *Dateline Jobs* shows more job postings for sales-related jobs than for any other group of employees other than "producer."

High Need! High Demand! Low Profile

Despite the high demand for salespeople, let me illustrate how low on the professional scale those outsiders continue to view the sales profession. So low that I was recently forced to talk back to my TV as I watched one of my favorite morning business TV programs, *Mornings with Maria,* on Fox Business.

Two hosts and two guests discussed the number of emerging technologies that currently use artificial intelligence and robotics, and their effects on business and economics. They flashed a graphic on the television screen that read,

> "45% of all occupations have the potential to become outdated."
>
> — *Tiger Tyagarajan, CEO of Genpact*

At one point, Maria said, "Robots are taking over jobs once held by humans, threatening the nature of most professions...I mean, you don't have emotion with robots. What about that emotion-oriented job? Are there any jobs that are safe from AI?"

I was surprised when the hosts and panelists looked around at each other and stammered as they tried to come up with ideas. They rambled on, and, just before the commercial break, one of them came up with—art! Yeah! Artists!

How about maybe ***sales?*** I told my TV set, *"None of you on-air guys would have your jobs if they weren't paid for by revenues produced by ad reps who sell your network's air time to sponsor your show!"*

So What?

Here's the bottom line:

Take heart.

With sales, you can create the best Return on Investment of any profession.

As long as products and services are bought by humans, they will be sold by humans.

The career that provides the least security short term is the most secure career of all long term: sales.

— Law of the Hired Gun

Why We Do This

One Halloween afternoon, the last day of the third month, I turned in the biggest deal in the history of one of the highest revenue-producing divisions in our company. Shortly after, my phone rang, and my favorite executive in the company said, "I just wanted to call so I can personally congratulate you on your deal! Especially today, the last day of the quarter. We weren't close to hitting our overall company number for the month, but your deal just came in and put the entire company way over the top!"

I really didn't know what to say, so I just kept listening. He continued, "I want to tell you what that means to me. Because of your deal putting the entire company over the top, I get to go home early this afternoon so I can take my daughters trick-or-treating downtown! And it's all because of your deal. So, I just wanted to say, congratulations—and thanks!"

I was so taken aback I really didn't know what to say. My mind instantly flashed back to the movie Burt Lancaster made about Jim Thorpe. King Gustav of Sweden tells Jim Thorpe on the podium of the 1912 Olympic Games, "You are the greatest athlete in the world!" The greatest athlete in the world merely replies, "Thanks, King."

My whole event, of course, doesn't rank anywhere within the universe of Thorpe's accomplishment, but I've long considered Jim Thorpe to be the greatest Olympian of all time, and his reaction to this compliment is what came to mind as I fumbled to find a reply. Rather ineloquently but just as sincerely, I simply said, "Thank you. That means a lot to me." But as I cradled my phone I felt as if Joe was standing there talking to me:

Thoughts produce feelings;
Feelings produce emotions;
Emotion is a powerful energy inside you that produces Motion;
The more Motion you have, the more people you can help;
The more people you help, the better life you can lead;
And it all comes back to the thoughts that occupy your mind.

— Joseph J. Charbonneau & Law of the Hired Gun

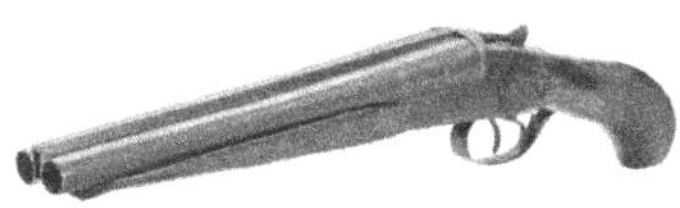

Levity Break

The Fisherman and the Banker

An investment banker took a much-needed vacation in a coastal Central American village when a small boat with just one fisherman docked. The boat had several large, fresh fish in it.

The investment banker was impressed by the quality of the fish.

He asked the fisherman how long it took to catch them.

The fisherman replied, "Only a little while."

The banker then asked why he didn't stay out longer and catch more fish?

The fisherman replied he had enough to support his family's needs.

The banker then asked, "But what do you do with the rest of your time?"

The fisherman replied, "I sleep late, fish a little, play with my children, take siesta with my wife, stroll into the village each evening where I sip wine and play guitar with my amigos: I have a full and busy life, señor."

The investment banker scoffed, "I am an Ivy League MBA, and I could help you. You could spend more time fishing and with the proceeds buy a bigger boat, and with the proceeds from the bigger boat you could buy several boats until eventually you would have a whole fleet of fishing boats. Instead of selling your catch to the middleman you could sell directly to the processor, eventually opening your own cannery. You could control the product, processing, and distribution."

Then he added, "Of course, you would need to leave this small coastal fishing village and move to a much bigger city where you would run your growing enterprise."

The fisherman asked, "But señor, how long will this all take?"

To which the banker replied, "15-20 years."

"But what then?" asked the fisherman.

The vacationing banker laughed and said, "That's the best part. When the time is right you would announce an IPO and sell your company stock to the public, and become very rich. You could make millions."

"Millions, señor? Then what?"

To which the banker replied, "Then you would retire! You could move to a small coastal fishing village where you would sleep late, fish a little, play with your kids, take siesta with your wife, stroll to the village in the evenings where you could sip wine and play your guitar with your amigos."

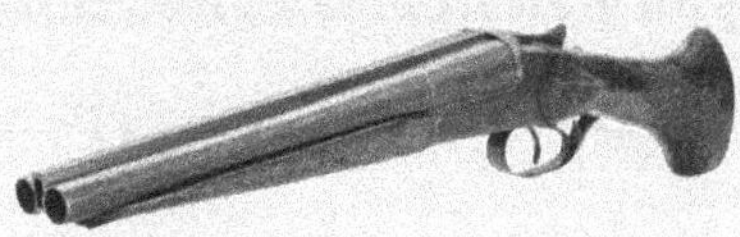

STAY TUNED! More to come from the Hired Gun!

REVENGE of the HIRED GUN®

In which we make a successful one-on-one sales call on The Boss, examine how sales success often leads to starting a new business and the nature of that phenomenal creature called the American Entrepreneur, interview three of the best salespeople you will ever read about plus one Financial Suit who maintains a genuine respect for his sales teams—and how they all grew from sales into entrepreneurs.

Dedication

To: Snarf - Little Big (Thunder) Cat

The Hired Gun Suggested Reading List:

Jeffrey Gitomer - *The Little Red Book of Selling: 12.5 Principles of Sales Greatness*
Stanley Marcus - *Minding the Store*
Carl Sewell - *Customers for Life: How to Turn That One-Time Buyer into a Lifetime Customer*
Donald J. Trump and Tony Schwartz - *The Art of the Deal*
David Sandler - *You Can't Teach a Kid to Ride a Bike at a Seminar*
J. Martin Kohe - *Your Greatest Power*
Dr. Eric Berne - *Games People Play: The Basic Handbook of Transactional Analysis*
Thomas Harris - *I'm OK - You're OK*
Gene Simmons - *On Power: My Journey Through the Corridors of Power and How You Can Get More Power*
Marcus Buckingham and Curt Coffman - *First, Break All the Rules: What the World's Greatest Managers Do Differently*
Chris Hogan - *Retire Inspired*

CPSIA information can be obtained
at www.ICGtesting.com
Printed in the USA
FFHW020606131219
56864480-62517FF

9 780966 666809